I0142489

REFORMED EPISTEMOLOGY

The relation of *LOGOS* and *RATIO*
in the history of Western epistemology

REFORMED EPISTEMOLOGY

The relation of *LOGOS* and *RATIO*
in the history of Western epistemology

Dirk H. T. Vollenhoven

Translation and introduction by Anthony Tol

Edited by John H. Kok

DORDT COLLEGE PRESS

Cover design by Rob Haan
Layout by Carla Goslinga

Copyright © 2013 Anthony Tol

Fragmentary portions of this book may be freely used by those who are interested in sharing the authors' insights and observations, so long as the material is not pirated for monetary gain and so long as proper credit is visibly given to the publisher and the author. Others, and those who wish to use larger sections of text, must seek written permission from the publisher.

Dordt College Press   www.dordt.edu/dordt_press
498 Fourth Avenue NE
Sioux Center, Iowa, 51250
United States of America

ISBN: 978-0-932914-98-9

Printed in the United States of America

The Library of congress Cataloguing-in-Publication Date is on files with the library of Congress, Washington D.C.

Library of Congress Control Number: 2013956705

Title of the original text: Logos en Ratio: Beider verhouding in de geschiedenis der westersche kentheorie (Kampen: J.H. Kok, 1926).
(Logos *and* Ratio: *Their relation in the history of Western epistemology*)

Address given upon accepting the chair of professor in the Faculty of Arts and Philosophy at the *Vrije Universiteit* of Amsterdam on Tuesday 26 October 1926. The full text in Dutch is available at: http://dare.ubvu.vu.nl/handle/1871/19185

TABLE OF CONTENTS

ACKNOWLEDGEMENTS

I wish to thank the board of the Vollenoven foundation for support and encouragement as I worked at this translation project. Distinct mention goes to K.A. Bril, R.A. Nijhoff, E.A. de Boer, and C. Gousmett, who all showed special interest in this project.

The translator also wishes to thank Gerben Groenewoud for his help with the Latin quotations both in the text and the footnotes. The translation and the general introduction also benefitted greatly from the critical and thorough reading by the editor John H. Kok.

A more oblique acknowledgement – more like an announcement – is the notification of a more recent use of the term "Reformed epistemology." This term again came into use in the late 1970s in the United States, particularly around the work of Alvin Plantinga and Nicolas Wolterstorff. This group too sees itself as operating within the Calvinist tradition, though it distinguishes itself from the earlier developments of neo-Calvinism, to which Vollenhoven contributed in the Netherlands, by seeking inspiration from the common-sense philosophy that began with Thomas Reid in the eighteenth century in Scotland. In this connection the volume, *Rationality in the Calvinian Tradition*, edited by H. Hart, J. van der Hoeven, and N. Wolterstorff (Lanham: University Press of America, 1983) is worthy of mention, for it contains the papers of a conference on the theme of rationality, held in August of 1981, in which representatives of both trends exchanged their points of view. In the attempt to clarify Vollenhoven's own views in the current work I thought it best to limit the discussion entirely to Vollenhoven's own neo-Calvinist contribution. Dutch readers, who are unacquainted with the more recent trend in epistemology within the "Presbyterian" wing of the Calvinian tradition, may consult, *De kentheorie van Alvin Plantinga*, edited by R. van Woudenberg and B. Cusveller (Zoetermeer: Boekencentrum, 1998).

Anthony Tol

Translator's note

The occasion, context, and meaning of the text here translated are discussed in the translator's "General introduction." The text on which the translation is based is the printed version. No manuscript version has been found to date, nor is there a printed version with corrections or revisions in Vollenhoven's hand. The occasional misprints that occur in the printed text could be corrected in an evident way, but unfortunately several lacunae in the text remain.

The text, which is itself rather challenging, has been embellished somewhat to make it more accessible. (i) The paragraphs have been numbered to facilitate reference. This does not disturb the "flow" of the text, for most paragraphs tend to be relatively self-contained. (ii) Some long paragraphs have been broken, where feasible, into subparagraphs. The latter are distinguished from Vollenhoven's own paragraph division in *lacking* both a reference number and an extra white space with the prior subparagraph. (iii) Subheadings, also included in an added "Table of Contents," have been incorporated (without square brackets) to make the topical divisions of this otherwise unmarked text more evident. (iv) Vollenhoven's rather free use of the colon – some sentences have as many as three colons – has often been replaced by a period when that is appropriate, or by an alternative expression, such as "namely," "for," etc. (v) Many persons are referred to solely by their surnames. Where feasible— the names of persons of antiquity being the exception – personal names or initials have been added (without square brackets). (vi) Vollenhoven's original text had no index.

The footnotes occurred initially as endnotes. Many of the authors referred to have today receded behind the horizon. But the footnotes reveal Vollenhoven's sources; herein lies their importance. ♦

The translator has added a postscript about a particularly trying episode in Vollenhoven's relation with the *Vrije Universiteit* in the second

---

♦A case in point: when consulting Richard Herbertz, *Prolegomena zu einer realistischen Logik* (Halle: M. Niemeyer, 1916) in the library of the *Vrije Universiteit*—see footnote 7 in the main text—I found that pages 1–195 of this 221 page book still showed Vollenhoven's characteristic marginal markings and underscored words!

half of the 1930s. This postscript is included, not only as call for reha-
bilitation of his unjust treatment, but also to show how confrontational
the critical discussion of scholasticism was at this institution at the time.

The first priority of this translation is to offer an accurate rendition of Vollenhoven's thought. The expression of this in his characteristic
"chiselled style" does not lead to smooth literary reading even in his own
language. Style has had to bow to text fidelity in this translation as well.

Anthony Tol

GENERAL INTRODUCTION

A. *Introduction*

This English-language text is the author's inaugural address, in translation from the Dutch, which he delivered when he accepted the first full-time appointment in philosophy at the *Vrije Universiteit* of Amsterdam on 26 October 1926.

In the on-going project of making the main works of Vollenhoven more internationally accessible, this address cannot be passed by. An inaugural address is usually an occasion on which the appointee discloses something of the nature of his work and what he hopes to accomplish. Important in this connection is also the relevance of the appointment for the institution. What will the effect of the appointment be? How will it benefit the (forty-six year old) university?

The events of that day are, of course, now more than three quarters of a century behind us and the current reader glances back and sees a time with concerns that in many ways are no longer ours. But as an historical topic the situation at the time can be assessed in a way that the actuality of that moment could not have revealed. What did Vollenhoven place on the agenda by giving this address, what is its importance in connection with the author's general standpoint, and does it still have meaning for us today? It is only fair that the reader should have the opportunity – for which this translation provides – of confronting the text with serious inquiry. These pages are meant to introduce the text and give the reader a head start.

B. *The inauguration*

The appointment and inauguration were significant for both the appointee, Dirk Hendrik Theodoor Vollenhoven (1892–1978), and the *Vrije Universiteit* of Amsterdam. For Vollenhoven – to mention his personal gain first – it allowed him the opportunity to devote himself full-time to philosophy. He was granted the Ph.D. in philosophy at the *Vrije Universiteit* in 1918 with a dissertation on the philosophy of mathematics "from a theistic standpoint."[1] His standpoint was programmatic, implying that more areas of knowledge could be organized within that same framework[2] – a framework that he hoped to develop in the years ahead.[3] But for the next eight years he was a pastor in two Reformed churches and his involvement in philosophy had to be more or less restricted to spare time activity. His appointment to the chair of philosophy, Vollenhoven states in his closing words, "resolved the great tension in which I have lived the last years" (§214).[4] Now he could devote all of his time to teaching philosophy and further research.

The appointment had important ramifications for the institution as well. With this appointment the *Vrije Universiteit* was devoting for the first time a full-time position to philosophy. While philosophy had not been neglected,[5] the piecemeal attention given to it since the university's

---

1 Vollenhoven 1918a; the title, translated, is "The philosophy of mathematics from a theistic standpoint." For a detailed discussion of this work, cf. Kok 1992, also Tol 2010, chapter 2.

2 Cf. in this regard Stellingwerff 1992: 25.

3 Cf. Vollenhoven's letter to A. Janse, 19 February 1924, in Tol 2010: 244 n.44.

4 References to the inaugural address (bibliographic code: 1926a) use the numbered paragraphs of that text. Other texts of Vollenhoven are referred to by the respective code reference in the bibliography on pages xlviii–xlix.

5 Cf. Klapwijk 1980: 529–553; see also §212.

founding in 1880 did hinder the realization of the aims of the university as a Reformed institution, aims that it was wont to express in terms of "the Reformed principles" ["*Gereformeerde beginselen*"]. When the university addressed its Reformed identity in a published report in 1895 it mentioned the importance of a (modern) theory of knowledge and related topics, *provided* that this core philosophical discipline could be developed in a Reformed way (cf. §212).[6] In other words, at the turn of the twentieth century the *Vrije Universiteit* was underscoring the importance of the *ideal* of a "Reformed epistemology." But it took another quarter century before the conditions necessary to implement this ideal were put into operation with a full-time appointment in philosophy.

The choice of Vollenhoven for this position seemed to be just right. The "theistic standpoint" that was operational in the dissertation of 1918 was in line with the university's 1895 adumbration of "Reformed epistemology," although Vollenhoven made no mention of this document at the time. In his dissertation he defended what he calls a "qualified scholastic" position. Below we will pause to see how this qualified scholastic or theistic position in fact comports with essential features advocated in the university report. With the inaugural address we seem to be in the same slipstream, if we take the terms of the title – "*logos*" and "*ratio*" – at face value. But looks, especially *prima facie* ones, can deceive. One finds on further review that there is a striking *discontinuity* between the main thrust of the address and Vollenhoven's prior published work. In fact, the very "theistic standpoint" is criticized, though without Vollenhoven's *explicitly* mentioning the application to his own former work and attitude. As it turns out the new professor of philosophy is announcing and referring to a *revised* "Reformed epistemology" as compared to that defended in his early work. This is daring, also in light of the university's epistemic ideal (as expressed in the report of 1895) that Vollenhoven now no longer completely shares.[7] In fact, the inaugural address is the first general statement of what Vollenhoven will from now on defend as being "Reformed

---

6   Cf. Woltjer and Kuyper 1895; in translation the title of this report reads: "Publication of the Senate of the *Vrije Universiteit* regarding the investigation towards determining the way that leads to the knowledge of the Reformed principles"; cf. also Tol 2010: 42–55, which mentions the epistemological themes involved.

7   In Vollenhoven 1926d: 191–192, the author explicitly criticizes the epistemology of his much respected former mentor, Jan Woltjer, one of the authors of the university report. Vollenhoven is critical of Woltjer's basing epistemology on the "subject–object structure," a position he shared in his own earlier work. Now, from 1926 on, Vollenhoven bases epistemology on (what might be called) the "subject-truth-object structure." See our discussion below.

philosophy."[8]

C. *The standpoint of "Reformed philosophy"*

The title "Reformed philosophy" is for Vollenhoven, first and foremost, an indication of where he chooses to situate his standpoint in connection with philosophy.[9] Its locus is the tradition of the Reformation in its Reformed branch. In practical terms this means that this tradition is taken as being capable of providing conditions for philosophical thought, conditions that *situate* philosophy in life as a whole – here the Reformed religious condition has its say – and that *orientate* philosophical reflection in line with relevant worldview distinctions regarding our life's practice in the world. To be more explicit, as to the religious condition, Vollenhoven finds this best formulated in the Reformed context of "covenant theology," here understood not as a theological construal but as living existentially and ineluctably in the presence of God (§77). The focus of this presence is expressed in the love command (to love God above all and our neighbor as ourselves; cf. Mark 12: 29–31). Though the human response – essential to religion – is positive or negative, one cannot nullify one's "standing in subjection" to the demand of the love command (or religion in general). The worldview relevance, in turn, comes to the fore in the choice for what Abraham Kuyper called "sphere sovereignty" (§209). This endorses an anti-totalitarian view of life-practice. It advocates a spread of the exercise of power and authority over the diversity of offices of responsibility, which offices at the same time limit relevant power deployment and authority. "Life-rules" govern the practice taking place within a sphere, making concrete that the "standing in subjection" involves all creatures.

Now philosophy needs to consider its presuppositions. The reflec-

---

8   In the same year as the inaugural address (1926a) Vollenhoven published two articles, entitled (in translation) "Contours of the theory of knowledge" (1926b) and "Theory of knowledge and natural science" (1926d). John Kok has rightly observed that the three publications (1926a, 1926b, and 1926d) "together constitute a closely orchestrated epistemological statement with explicitly formulated ontological underpinnings. In fact, the three are so much of a unit that any one of them cannot be understood well without the other two" (Kok 1992: 233). In our discussion below we shall also refer to these two articles. We add that Vollenhoven's (unpublished) lecture notes of 1926–1927 (1926msA) are relevant as well.

9   Vollenhoven always spoke of "Calvinistic philosophy." In 1926d: 189 he describes his work as "Calvinistic theory of knowledge." Given the near equivalence of "Reformed" to "Calvinistic" either term is a viable option. The term "Reformed" has the advantage of avoiding unwelcome confusions with John Calvin, who was a theologian not a philosopher.

tion in which this takes place must be distinguished from its own critical and constructive thought practice. Were this not the case, then philosophy's presuppositions would turn into direct suppositions of thought and be adjudicated within the trends of that thought. This would in turn call for a recognition of new presuppositions to illuminate the relevance of that thought process. But then there is no reason not to treat the new presuppositions in the same way, and one ends up with an unending regression. To reflect on presuppositions is not to do constructive philosophy, but it is to search for the link between what one accepts as philosophy's task and possibilities of meaningful conditions for its execution.[10]

This means that the "standpoint" of Reformed philosophy is not itself a part of philosophy for Vollenhoven – it doesn't formulate (say) its "axioms" – but it delineates what "Reformed" is to mean in connection with doing philosophy. In this connection two misunderstandings need to be avoided. What is it to refer to "the whole of reality" when speaking of situating philosophy in life as a whole, and what is it to appeal to "relevant worldview distinctions" in connection with the orientation of philosophy? Both of these notions are reckoned as being relevant as presuppositions.

As to the first point, "the whole" is not meant as a distinct form of being, something in itself, apart from God and the world (though perhaps including both). Rather for Vollenhoven "the whole" ineluctably involves God in that nothing can be that is apart from God, God being the source of all. One speaks more specifically of God's transcendence in connection with the (law-)conditions imposed by him on the world, and thus also on human life. The impingement of these conditions in the world and human life attests to God's immanence (in a transcendental sense). The covenantal "walking with God" makes this concrete in God's expectation that the human being images him in all the activities of life "for good." Religion, in turn, is the encompassing *life-attitude* in which human actuality takes place, evincing the qualification of being either "for good or ill" in the face of what the biblical love command entails. Thus "activity evincing good or evil" characterizes "the whole" as God-maintained. The evidence is indirect, but it seems that Vollenhoven had only recently come to understand Calvinism in this way prior to 1926.[11]

---

10   Cf. my "Vollenhoven on Philosophy, Worldview, and Religion," to appear on the website of the Vollenhoven Foundation.

11   With respect to the view of Calvinism that Vollenhoven now espouses, he wrote, late 1926 in an unpublished note, of having undergone a "rather drastic" change in his understanding of Calvinism (cf. Tol 2010: 381). In §77 Vollenhoven formulates a "short summary" on the relation of religion and theology. Vollenhoven did not

As to the second point, the "worldview distinctions" give latitude to activity. The doctrine of sphere sovereignty emphasizes that the activity of creatures is not to be understood as bound to one type of ordinance. Concrete living evidences a need to differentiate between different kinds of ordinances – Vollenhoven speaks uniformly of "laws" – and thus law-bound activity is likewise diverse. This is what gives way to speaking of "law-spheres," in which the most basic kinds of law-bound activity are organized and specified. This provides the context for the qualification "for good or ill," as relevant to each law-sphere; although Vollenhoven only comes to make this explicit in the early 1930s.[12] In our present context Vollenhoven resorts (somewhat unfortunately) to speaking of "metaphysics" (e.g., §20). He uses this term to emphasize the "intersection" of every creature with law-spheres, as life-contexts in which creatures stand and act. To presuppose this "intersection principle" as the matrix of sphere sovereignty is to confess to a diversity laid in creation itself. It "prepares" the way for cosmology (§126) and epistemology. Vollenhoven maintained this principle throughout his later career.

What accompanies both covenant religion and the worldview of sphere sovereignty is Scripture, in Vollenhoven's Calvinistic reading of it (especially in view of the "boundary" problem between God and the world). Scriptural authority is an important factor for Vollenhoven in determining the meaning of the presuppositions of philosophy. He says little in defense of the relation of Scripture revelation and philosophy in this address. But he emphasizes in his personal word that the relevance of the Christian faith "is entailed in the foundation of the critique implied in the historical overview presented to you this afternoon" (§212). Vollenhoven appears to prefer this formulation over one that specifically mentions "Reformed principles."

D. *Scholasticism and humanism*

Indeed, apart from advocating his own understanding of epistemology in this inaugural address Vollenhoven voices criticism as to how epistemol-

---

immediately have a clear terminology in consequence of his changed view. In the current address (and into the 1930s) he speaks of the "pure dualism" of God and cosmos, as opposed to "impure" forms and particularly holistic (or "monistic") views (§§9–10); cf. also Tol 2010, chapter 4 for an explanatory and critical discussion. In his dissertation of 1918 he had spoken of "Christian dualism" as pertaining to the contrast: norm/freedom versus fact/necessity (1918: 2–3), a formulation influenced by scholasticism (see below).

12   See my general introduction (in Dutch) to Vollenhoven 2010.

ogy is generally understood. The critique is cast in a historical overview.[13] Vollenhoven is particularly critical of two features that were prominent in philosophy at the time of his address and in the first half of the twentieth century, namely, *scholasticism* and *humanism*. These features, however, have a relevance throughout philosophy's history, though the terminology in which this is expressed changes with time.

Scholasticism, in the sense here meant, turns the religious presupposition of philosophy into an ontological feature of reality itself. It postulates the reality of a *sacred* realm over against a *secular* one. In other words, "the whole" is taken to be dualistic, but in an "improper" sense. Especially improper is the *contrast* or *opposition* it induces in the understanding of created reality. Vollenhoven's "Reformed" understanding of "God and the world" is that the created world is dependent in its entirety on God's sovereignty. This distinction of dependence and sovereignty is, to be sure, also a duality, but it is emphatically not oppositional nor contrasting. The divine relevance comes into its own in religious life, "in its full [i.e., all-inclusive] concreteness,"[14] also as regards the human being. This induces philosophy to consider the world and the human being from an integral perspective. However, in scholasticism, anthropology is made to fit the oppositional or contrasting mold of the sacred and the secular. The human being is seen as participating in both realms. In predisposing this possibility, the human being is thought to consist of the dualism of an immortal soul and a mortal body. Vollenhoven believes that this does not do justice to the complex (cosmic) unity of the human being.

Humanism is also a prime feature of historically relevant philosophy that Vollenhoven criticizes. Humanism interprets the responsibility that the human being has for his acts and dealings with his fellow beings and the world as essentially derived from self-responsibility. The human Self is taken as having primary value in being the basis of the moral law and thus as the judge of good and evil (cf. §§170 ff.). This sentiment found much support in the (Neo-)Idealism of the 1920s and 1930s. Today the appeal to human autonomy has lost much of its attraction, and in some cases has made way for the priority of heteronomy.[15] Does this outdate

---

13 The nature of such a critical discussion is conducted according to what Vollenhoven soon came to call "the thetical-critical method." This method, usually applied intuitively, guides Vollenhoven's practice of philosophy. The "thetical" part is based on intuited insight; the "critical" part usually takes on the form of historical review. Vollenhoven anticipates this method in §5. For discussion of this method (and two more specific methods), cf. Tol 2010, chapter 1, and Tol 2011b.

14 Vollenhoven 2005e: §115, also §§25, 95.

15 This is particularly so in the case of Emmanuel Levinas, who studied philosophy in

Vollenhoven's discussion? Not essentially, for responsibility, taken in a heteronymous sense, is entirely in line with Vollenhoven's appeal to the religious covenant.[16] The latter is the context in which the human being is aware of being endowed with responsibility, the actualization of which takes place in law-spheres of normed activity. (Heteronomy is also to be preferred to the relativism that postmodernism often evinces.) We will see that Vollenhoven also generalizes the relevance of humanism. It is not restricted to modern versions of Idealism.

The terms "scholasticism" and "humanism" are the prime foci of Vollenhoven's criticism. It is not coincidental that he ends his academic discussion with Husserl. Husserl is portrayed as caught in a web of humanism ("creative Ego"; "idealism") and a version of scholasticism (see §205). This is not so much due to his personal idiosyncrasy (though naturally he has made his choices in this regard), as to being the effect of his standing in a long tradition. Vollenhoven counters this not only in the interest of "the free development of epistemology" (§208), but also to forewarn Christian academics to withstand the temptations of synthesis with scholasticism and/or humanism, and to understand Christendom as calling for a different development, one that is informed and encouraged by different presuppositions (see §§209–212).[17] Vollenhoven continued to advocate this throughout his whole career.

E. *Scholasticism and humanism in schemata*

Vollenhoven's focusing on the terms "scholasticism" and "humanism" seems to lack generality. Each has, after all, its own highpoint of expression: scholasticism in the Middle Ages and humanism in the modern period. But Vollenhoven does not limit his use of these terms in this way. In fact they become the *main parameters* of his criticism when generalized to include prior formations and when brought to bear in different formulations and differences of nuance.

---

a setting in which Neo-Idealism was prominent. Later he resolutely took ethics to be primary philosophy, the appeal of the other – hence heteronomy – thereby being the heart of ethics; cf. P. Nemo's long interview with Levinas on central themes of the latter's thought in Levinas 1985.

16 Vollenhoven 2005e: §112, comment 3. "Heteronomy" here is more than just the acknowledgement of a "law-source" in the other; it includes recognition of the source in God: "theonomy."

17 Here again the thetical-critical method is at work (see note 13 above). The method is mentioned and discussed for the first time in the opening sections of *Isagôgè Philosophiae*. The latter text is Vollenhoven's introduction to philosophy, the first complete version of which, in syllabus format, is from 1930; cf. Vollenhoven 2005d, 2005e, and 2010.

What we see is that the term "scholasticism" goes proxy for a view or reading of one of the primary features of reality, a reading reflected in "the sacred and the secular," namely, as an *ontology of reality*. It depicts, in a *vertical* arrangement, an intrinsic difference of worth in the main parts of reality. It came to this, Vollenhoven here maintains, via the classical distinction of essence and appearance. In Plato this distinction is oppositional: essence is the higher and separate principle of *being*, hidden behind the appearances that are rated lower. The latter have an intrinsic feature of *non-being* (cf. §§18ff). However in Aristotle the two notions form the bi-unity of a contrast: the essence resides in the *form* that controls the *material* appearance as shaped by the form. Vollenhoven speaks of the Aristotelian all-inclusive "pyramid formation" of matter (or material) and form (cf. §26). Between the lowest formless matter (the potential) and the highest immaterial form – the latter is the (sacred!) self-consciousness of deity, expressed as "thought thinking itself" – we find different shades of the combination of form and matter to account for plant, animal, and human structures.

When referring to such a vertical, all-inclusive ontology of reality, in whatever variant relevant to the discussion (oppositional or contrasting), Vollenhoven uses the shorthand notation of "the form-matter schema" (also "form-material schema"). This expression should not be limited to the strictly Aristotelian mold. Vollenhoven takes it as a metaphor denoting the *vertical dimension of* (the structure of) *reality* as such, irrespective of how this is conceived in its details. But the schema is also meant to express criticism. It refers to a questionable ontology, especially when it encourages taking different attitudes to different parts of reality: e.g., veneration of what is higher and disdain for what is lower in their vertical arrangement.[18] In this sense this includes scholasticism, in its historically more limited sense, as important exemplar.

Vollenhoven finds the effect of this schema also reflected in epistemology, in particular in what he calls the abstraction theory. Thomas Aquinas maintains that at the sensory level there is no knowledge to speak of. The imagination, by abstracting from the sensory data, brings about an internal material, from which the intellect abstracts what is

---

18   We wish to observe that this ontology can be appealed to sociologically to justify the scapegoat mechanism. The latter is the operation that sacrifices what is of low esteem for the welfare and purity of what is of higher value, as René Girard has demonstrated so forcefully (Girard 1986; also Tol 2011b). The scapegoat mechanism can also be applied anthropologically to justify suppressing bodily needs for the greater glory of mental achievement (as in Nietzsche and Freud). We find an example of the latter in the early Vollenhoven; see below, section G.3, pp. xxv ff.

considered knowable (see §72). Kant too is seen as maintaining sensory, imaginational, and intellectual levels, against a background that reflects an Aristotelian metaphysics (cf. §143).[19]

"Humanism" follows suit. This term, when used as a generalized parameter, serves to describe the (all-inclusive) *horizontal dimension* of the human being in interaction with the world (or environment), in which the human element is depicted as being most prominent. Vollenhoven speaks of "a typical Western appraisal of the human being" in connection with the "dualism of subject and object" (§12). The original motive operative here is not as yet "self-responsibility" but the problem of the control of the environment, in particular as evidenced in language use. The subject subjects, to which the object objects (§14).

Western epistemology is predicated on this dualism. Despite its being so historically entrenched Vollenhoven is very critical in his appraisal. Ever since Socrates epistemology has proceeded from this dualism, taking it to be its essential model (§16). Beginning with perception, subject and object have a natural "horizontal orientation" in that, in an obvious sense, we first see the objects around us. When advancing to knowledge, we reckon with the measure to which the object is known by the subject (now taken as knowing agent) in specific acts. Believing, asserting, judging, conceiving, etc. are acts that each call for a corresponding content, as derived from the object. In this connection, too, Vollenhoven uses a shorthand expression in referring to this horizontal arrangement generally, namely, the "act-content schema." This schema expresses the human involvement (act) with the object, giving rise to grasped (mental) content.

But this schema hides an important problem. Knowledge differs from perception in calling for truth. But where does truth come from as we slide from perception to knowledge? It would appear to have its source somewhere in the act-content distinction. But this is typically seated in the knowing agent. At first (in the historical sense) truth seems

---

19　At this early moment in his career Vollenhoven had a broad but not as yet nuanced grasp of agreement and differences between thinkers that will characterize his later historical work, especially in the context of the problem-historical method. In the context of the latter method he finds more differences between Aristotle and Kant than are presumed here, also the "form-matter schema" (in its Aristotelian setting) is then interpreted as being oppositional instead of contrasting, as here. But this does not defeat the general argument of his address at this point. We note too a difference in the use of "monism"; in Vollenhoven's work up to the 1940s it is a synonym for "holism" (cf. §§9, 10, 16), in the problem-historical method it is the bi-unity of contrasting poles/moments/species, etc. From this latter perspective, the (1926) oppositional duality is "dualistic," the contrasting duality "monistic."

to be sought in terms of the analogy between the human being and the object (§§17, 18). But after the classical Greek period truth is postulated to be innate in the human mind (§46). Here we appear to have the primary reason for speaking of "humanism" (or some form of idealism).[20] Vollenhoven himself takes clear distance from this humanism of truth in accepting the *realism* of truth: it is a reality "in itself" (§87). We'll need to see what this means. Vollenhoven at least adamantly *disconnects* perception and knowledge – they are said to differ "diametrically" (§17; cf. also §§33, 115). All told, he entirely opposes the suggestion of truth being seated in the human subject.

Thus both the vertical and the horizontal dimensions, in their generalized forms and as traditionally understood, call for critical discussion, though Vollenhoven does not reject the relevance of these dimensions as such. They need rather to be seen as structured in a different way than as realized in scholasticism and humanism.

Now there is one further point. The vertical and the horizontal dimensions also intersect, which is of particular relevance in the human being (cf. §53). The latter's "horizontal" interaction with the world locks into the world's "vertical" structure, usually at some level relevant for the human being. A typical example of intersection is when *act* in itself touches *form*. E.g., when act "forms," "fashions," or typifies the content, then an act has itself become a principle of form. Also when form, in turn, is taken in an active sense, as is usual at the human level when the "higher" reality is itself active – as when speaking of (say) "active intelligence" – then this identification of act and form even sounds plausible. The intersection of the schemata gives rise to the shorthand expression "form-content schema." Vollenhoven prefers to interpret this too in a horizontal sense. So it becomes in fact an alternative expression for the "act-content schema" (§§53, 55, 72). As rule of thumb, a schema has a horizontal meaning when "content" occurs, vertical when "matter" (or "material") occurs.

Vollenhoven makes preferential use of these shorthand "schemata." This tends to be confusing when the reader fails to see the background in their being "schemata" of (generalized) scholasticism and humanism respectively. In a strictly philosophical sense they (schematically) depict the ontological and epistemological situations, distinguished through the

---

20   In the later problem-historical approach the defense of innate ideas, first found in Cicero, but probably not original with him, becomes the general "theme of the a priori," a characteristic shared in most time-currents since the time of Roman philosophy; cf. under the index item "A priori, theory of" in Vollenhoven 2005b: 171.

formalism of "vertical" and "horizontal" arrangements. We now need to put this to work and see it in action. Doing so we hit upon the two key notions of Vollenhoven's address: "*logos*" and "*ratio*."

F. *Logos* and *ratio*

All of the foregoing is but a preparation to get to what Vollenhoven wants to offer: a substantive discussion of epistemology. The main handles for this discussion are the two terms "*logos*" and "*ratio*." It will probably remain a mystery why Vollenhoven didn't introduce these terms more clearly than he does (cf. §§7–10). Of course, the terms themselves are ambiguous, in the sense of being manifold in their meaning. That meaning only unfolds as the historical discussion progresses. But, when taking stock of the whole discussion, some features do stand out.

1. *Logos*

The term "logos" is the Greek word for "word" or "speech," hence it necessarily involves language. It is the context of language that gives the term its punch. When speaking one is usually not merely reciting words; rather one is asserting or judging, or perhaps one is describing, prescribing, commanding, exclaiming, praying, denying, or doing a host of other things with words. Language is at its most dynamic when language use directly affects reality. Think of the general's command to attack or retreat, or of the verdict of the judge who pronounces the sentence of death or freedom, or the recital of the poet that moves or bores us. Thus "logos" is "*effective* word" or "*authoritative* speech." It is also in that capacity that it is important to logic, for the latter calls for a reasoning that is effective, aimed at offering argumentation with conviction.[21]

But language can be effective only if reality responds in kind. (You teach your child to speak but not your dog.) Here the "vertical dimension" (as discussed above) comes into the picture. If I take reality to be characterized by the ontology of (say) "the sacred and the secular," then that empowers my sense of (self-)evidence and effects what I take to be reasonable when assuming some definite operating quality. Or I could take the ontology of "life and death," as, say, Aristotle did; then *life* is taken in a teleological and goal-directed sense, and *death* denotes the absence of these qualities in passivity, inertness, "mere matter" (§39). But then the more complex forms of life – that entail responsibility, which organic life does not – such as social life, economic life, religious life, etc.,

---

21   For Heraclitus this is the sole way of understanding the *logos*. The efficacy of the *logos* is the direct strife provided by the very process that makes effective (see §13).

are primarily approached and understood as modeled on organic life. Also associating matter with death has its problems: matter we now know is energy and process! In general one may say that, from ancient philosophy on, what makes for understanding reality is the *logos* as general "form" suggested by the ontology of reality. The general form is grasped as being the feature that is effective in virtue of the fundamental opposition or contrast in reality itself, whether this be as "essence" over against "appearance" or as "(operational) form" in bi-unity with "matter" (or variations of these kinds of ontology). The *logos* is the feature of efficacy in its most general sense, which, when grasped, is the basis of intelligence.

Vollenhoven's own position in this regard, which he "posits" and gradually unfolds as the analysis progresses, is to hold that the intelligibility of reality is itself specifically structured. Intelligibility is warranted by a *distinct* basic feature of reality, which feature is on a par with other basic features. These basic features are organized in "law-spheres" (spoken of earlier), one of which is essential for the *logos* itself. (In Vollenhoven's address the term "*logos*" gradually makes way for the phrase "logical law-sphere," the latter's first occurrence being in §66.)

Now, about these law-spheres, they themselves form a (linear) "vertical dimension," like chapters of a well-organized book (§66). No one law-sphere is privileged over the others, apart from what follows from each law-sphere's own nature in the context of the whole vertical dimension. (In other words, this dimension is gradated in different kinds of reality, but not as based on conditions of worth.) The logical law-sphere (*logos*) is here taken to be the first or lowest sphere, with all the others "resting" on it in a vertical sense.[22] Thus the second law-sphere rests immediately on the logical law-sphere, the third one mediately, through its resting immediately on the second sphere, and so on up. The metaphor of "resting on the *logos*" means to express that something of the nature of the *logos* is reflected in the second law-sphere: it marks an *analogical* presence of the *logos* there. But in the third law-sphere there is also an analogy of the *logos*, though it is mediated through the second law-sphere. And

---

22 Its position as the first or foundational law-sphere was soon (cf. Vollenhoven 1926msA, which extends into 1927) changed to an approximately middle position of the vertical dimension of the law-spheres and was to remain there. We discuss some of the implications of this shift below (cf. H.4: New developments). The first reference to "pure logic" being in first position is in H. Dooyeweerd's unpublished paper, "Normatieve rechtsleer" ["Normative legal doctrine"] (1922: 36). This paper contains results that Dooyeweerd and Vollenhoven had come to in their discussions at the time (1921–1922). We add that the context in Dooyeweerd's text is metalogical (the context of the logic of the system of the sciences, not ontological as in Vollenhoven's work of 1926. Cf. Tol 2010: 307ff.

so on for every other higher law-sphere. This assures that there is "intelligibility" throughout the whole vertical dimension.

Analogical presence or relevance, we add, is not unique to the logical law-sphere. Everywhere in the vertical dimension where a law-sphere rests on a lower law-sphere, there is an analogy of the lower sphere in the higher one resting on it. E.g., on the second law-sphere, the numerical law-sphere, there rests all the other law-spheres above it, the third law-sphere (the spatial law-sphere) resting immediately on the second sphere, the others mediately. Hence there is (also) a numerical analogy in all these higher spheres (having to do with an essential pluralism within each of these higher spheres). The highest law-sphere, the pistical, lacks analogically reflection of itself because there is no higher law-sphere resting on it, though it includes the analogies of all the other law-spheres below it (on which it rests). Thus the theme of analogy is not itself logical but ontological, holding throughout the "vertical dimension" of being. It being something we find in, and not inflicted on, reality, Vollenhoven can only assume its presence by virtue of creation (§137).

It is important to realize that the arrangement of "*logos* and its analogies,"[23] or any other law-sphere and its analogies, does not constitute a contrasting or oppositional split in the vertical dimension as a whole; the said arrangement is the Reformed alternative to that understanding.

2. *Ratio*

The term "*ratio*" is somewhat easier to place, since this Latin term translates directly as "rational," "rationality," and the like. Rationality is for Vollenhoven first and foremost a matter that involves the human agent. It is a feature relevant to the human agent's coming to know and thus relevant to human knowledge acquisition. Vollenhoven links rationality to the *logos* in the sense that rationality basically involves the human *use* of what the *logos* provides (cf. e.g., §§66, 154). Rationality isn't thereby taken to be intrinsic to the human being as such – a presumed mental characteristic – but rather as intrinsic to the reality the human being strives to know. This "rational use" has to be executed "properly," therefore rationality presupposes a context of responsibility – hence rationality is not prior to responsibility. But the knowing subject's use gives different results when applied in different contexts of responsibility, the latter being apportioned over law-spheres. This implies that there is always the

---

23   Strictly speaking the *logos* includes the logical law-sphere and its analogies (also termed "states of affairs") in the other law-spheres (1926b: 397, 398). In use it sometimes seems to be a synonym for just the logical law-sphere.

relevance of responsibility matching that of a particular law-sphere. But how are we to understand all this?

Above, mention was made of the "intersection" of the human being and the law-spheres.[24] This is a way of stating that human living, activity, and practice take place in the context of distinct "spheres" of activity. The human situation is that the human being stands subject to the "laws" (or rules, ordinances, etc.) relevant to a sphere. All activity is law- or rule-bound. Thus the human being is never exempt from being in a normative situation, namely that of standing in subjection to rules. Human conscience betokens the awareness of this as *intuition*. We are aware of different kinds of activity – organic, lingual, social, economic, juridical, ethical, etc. – and also sense their being rule-bound to different rules, though we might be hard put to specify the rules explicitly. The rules become a part of the accepted traditions of culture. But in a dynamic society, new or adjusted rules are required to meet the challenge of changes of society. Thus our awareness on this score is always up for critical perusal.[25]

The human being also has a participatory (or intersecting) role in the logical law-sphere. Thus there is also an intuitive awareness as to what logic is "materially." Vollenhoven points here to *relational connection* as being of the essence of the logical law-sphere. As law-sphere it is "no more than a cosmic interrelationship of distinct character" (§153). (By implication this is what every law-sphere is formally.) So the fundamental logical situation is that of intuiting this cosmic coherence as involving, in a primitive sense, *relations* and *terms*. Together they constitute a system, and that system of relation-with-terms (as relata) is intuited as the logical form or the "logical schema."[26] In other words, through the intuition of

---

24   Cf. e.g., §20. Vollenhoven's language is not very perspicuous here. An individual is referred to as a "cosmic unity" and explained to be an "essence." Complex unities, such as humankind, social institutions, and the like, are also cosmic unities, which intersect with various law-spheres. Their being understood to be essences (Dutch: *wezens*) reminds one that essences are not unities hidden behind appearances but unities in their cosmic participation in law-spheres.

25   To intuit a law-sphere is to discern its law-bound *modal* character, i.e., its "(normative) mode of being," characteristic of fundamental existential practice. The result of such discerning is formulated as a "judgment of discerning" or "judgment of existence" (§§16, 20). This is the most primitive form (or "simplest type") of judgment (§§36, 199). Cf. further discussion below, section H.1, pp. xxxiii ff.

26   The logical schema is completely general. It can take on any specification so long as this is consistent with its structure as system (1926b: 397). We may note, though Vollenhoven makes no mention of this here, that the logical form is a system of a universal and particulars. At the "primitive" level, relations are always universals,

the logical schema the logical law-sphere makes available an instrument to the knowing subject. Intelligence, warranted by the *logos*, is modeled on understanding relational connection.

The actual *use* to which the logical schema is put involves being able to confront (in a horizontal sense) any non-logical law-sphere with the logical schema. Now each non-logical law-sphere has an analogy of the logical law-sphere, which is to say, in each there is a relational network. At the same time this network is qualified by the character of the law-sphere involved, i.e., each has relations and terms that are modulated to be in character with the modality of the law-sphere involved; e.g., in the numerical law-sphere, numerical relations and numerical terms; in the social law-sphere, social relations and social terms, etc. Vollenhoven calls what is intuited of these logical analogies "states of affairs." States of affairs represent in the logical modality the content of the logical analogy, the latter being a part of any non-logical law-sphere. The (horizontal) confrontation with the logical schema is meant to highlight or illuminate the relational structure in the state of affairs. Vollenhoven speaks of "encumbering the logical schema" with the relevant data of the state of affairs: objects ("*Gegenstände*") becoming terms, "essential connections" ("*wezensverbanden*") in the state of affairs becoming the relations, and the unity of the relational system being warranted by the "modality" (or mode of being) of the law-sphere in which the state of affairs occur. In other words, the use of the logical schema enables one to *understand* the state of affairs of a law-sphere as organized through a relational network. In that sense relational networks are the sounding board for thought, enabling one to come to know differences and connections relevant to a law-sphere (differences being indicated by the terms, connections by the relations).[27]

---

while particulars always carry their particularity with them. Every law-sphere has the two sides of universality and particularity, namely its own essential connection and terms respectively. (This is intrinsic to its "sphere"-part; the norm, as the "law-part," is distinct from this.) The logical law-sphere seizes on this, in its logical schema, as its most basic trait. In 1925 Vollenhoven had stated that the logical terrain "yields for us the logical essence par excellence, namely the 'relation'" (1925c: 393).

27   The "sphere"-part of the logical law-sphere would appear to be a "logic of relations," perhaps containing what A.N. Whitehead and B. Russell present in their Whitehead and Russell 1910; (cf. Part I, section D; pp. 231–301). This is at least compatible with Vollenhoven's claim that "there is a gamut of details to be noticed concerning the logical schema," adding in brackets: "(relation logic)" (1926d: 58–59). But Vollenhoven is completely silent about the "law"-part of the logical law-sphere. In his dissertation (1918a) he took the classical principles of logic to be norms or injunctions. This understanding appears to be essentially continued in the current context,

Thus the specific theme of rationality is how the person, as knowing subject, uses the form (or logical schema) in confrontation with content (state of affairs).[28] Vollenhoven's Reformed interpretation emphasizes in particular (i) the knowing subject's standing in subjection to norms as condition of rationality and (ii) the knowing subject's using the instrument of the *logos* – a completely passive instrument, this being a schema – to illuminate what is intelligible in the state of affairs. Through the synthesis of form and content, i.e., of logical schema and states of affairs, the knowing subject gets to grasp a *truth*. And *truth possessed is knowledge*. The humanist's alterative interpretation ignores the knowing subject's normed situation and looks to the logical form as a kind of "truth-maker" when working on perceived sensory material (as over against discerned modally diverse content). This humanistic approach attributes to the logical form a basic activity – a creative rationality – something Vollenhoven finds totally misplaced (§§141, 202).

We have not as yet discussed the epistemological notions – concepts and judgments – that "fit" the setup of *logos* and *ratio*, as discussed above, having only mentioned their intuitive base. But we can already provisionally conclude that Vollenhoven's "logic" is essentially *externalist*. Intelligibility is a built-in feature of reality as such, and only when the human being, as knowing subject, uses its (intelligibility's) possibility when coming into a proper rapport with states of affairs can satisfaction in understanding be expected, as rational quality.

G. *Theism as ideal: Vollenhoven's initial standpoint*

Before broaching Vollenhoven's (revised) Reformed epistemology more specifically, we ought first to discuss his attitude towards theism. He held to a "theistic ideal" in his early work, but it was an ideal he came to regret, at least in his early implementation of it. "But," one might ask, "how can

---

although these norms are no longer taken to be norms of truth (as was the case in 1918a). We note in passing that Vollenhoven does not refer to Russell at all in this connection, so our assuming the latter's indirect presence in the background remains speculative. But Vollenhoven was aware of his importance in connection with the theory of relations. He devoted almost 100 pages of critical discussion of Russell's work (up to about 1915) in his dissertation; cf. Vollenhoven 1918; pp. 241–338; cf. also Tol 2010: 104–108.

28 For a summary formulation of this in Vollenhoven, see his 1926d: 57–58. One might compare this with H. Dooyeweerd's later discussion of the (so-called) "Gegenstand-relation" in the context of his transcendental critique of theoretical thought (Dooyeweerd 1953: 38ff.). But because Dooyeweerd appeals to the supra-temporal Ego (transcendental Ego) in that critique, there is a substantial difference between his and Vollenhoven's epistemology at this point.

Reformed epistemology not be theistic?" Let it be said at once that it is not Vollenhoven's Christian faith – the faith in God – that is at stake, nor a relevance for epistemology. What is up for criticism is the way that divinity is (supposedly) available for epistemology in the scholastic tradition. In this connection Vollenhoven reported, in late 1926, that between 1918 and the time of writing his view as to what is characteristic of Calvinism had changed rather drastically (cf. footnote 11 above). He failed to say what the change involved, though he does state that it made it possible to contemplate, for the first time, a fruitful application of "the basic thoughts of a Calvinistic epistemology."[29] To get a handle on this, we need to touch on the essentials of Vollenhoven's initial epistemological position, though limitations of space demands that this be brief.[30]

1. *Knowledge and intuition*
For the early Vollenhoven, epistemology has two main chapters, one on *knowledge* and the other on *intuition*. Each supplements the other, without however either merging with or being subsumed under the other. This is warranted by the presupposition of the primary *duality of thought and being*. Thought, the seat of intuition, is nothing apart from being performed by the Self, based on an immediate insight. Being, in turn, involves the reality of the World, which is "alien to thought," a network of forces. It provides the given, the object, that the Self strives to know, beginning with perception.[31] Thought and being, or their embodiments in the activity of the Self and as regards the relevance of the World, come together in one perspective when we say that *when* experiencing (say, perceiving) an object we are aware *that* we are experiencing (per-

---

29   Vollenhoven 1926msC: 1; cf. also Tol 2010: 381ff.

30   Several (more extensive) summaries are available. Cf. Tol 2010: 211–216, 294, 362–364; Tol 2011: 192–199.

31   It is as yet an unanswered question how the young Vollenhoven came to accept this problematic distinction. We know that it is a fundamental distinction in F.A. Trendelenburg (1802–1872), whose influence extended into the twentieth century. As Erik Kreiter formulates it: "This fundamental contrast [between philosophical systems] is eventually construed by Trendelenburg as the opposition between thought (*Gedanke*) and 'blind,' or 'naked' force (*Kraft*). . . . But to constitute the fundamental difference, thought and the world must be taken in their greatest opposition. Being is most alien to thought. . . ." This agrees, in the very terminology, with Vollenhoven's early understanding; cf. Kreiter 2007: 18. An influence on Vollenhoven is likely, given that both J. Woltjer and W. Geesink used Trendelenburg's *Elementa logices aristotelicae* in their logic classes; cf. Woldring 2013: 32, 38. The distinction of being and thought is rightly rejected when seen as a case of mixing categories, such as (say) "being" and "validity"; cf. Vollenhoven 1926b: 388–389.

ceiving) and *that* content is involved (sense-data). Knowledge acquisition (the "when"-part) and intuition (the "that"-part) are quite distinct. Knowledge acquisition, beginning with perception, is piecemeal. It can be made more adequate to the object perceived through a build-up of many different representations of the object. But the knowledge gained is never complete, it never yields an "adequate concept" of the object. On the other hand, we are immediately aware through intuition that we are experiencing (sensing, representing, or remembering) when undergoing that experiencing, yielding content (sense-data, representations, and remembrances). Knowledge acquisition is arduous and subject to correction, while intuitive awareness is immediate and certain. The *genesis* of knowledge calls for the *justification* of intuition.

Looking more closely at knowledge, one can say that it is predicated on an object-to-subject relation. The object of the empirical world reveals itself to the Self in terms of its appearance. The Self absorbs this bodily through its psycho-physical organization, receiving the data in the context of the temporal and spatial forms of sensibility. The Self, being aware of this organized data, works this data into representations; and these in turn are used to form the predicates of judgments. In order for the Self to proceed to epistemological activity it needs to be aware of the *norms* that are relevant for that practice. This involves the mind's choice of abiding by the classical logical principles (of non-contradiction, identity, and excluded middle), which, functioning as norms, guide the genesis of knowledge. In this capacity the Self has taken on the attitude of "knowing subject," which includes a "will to know" and equally a will to avoid the waywardness of error. Hence, to acquire knowledge, data has to be received or ingested; in other words, knowledge cannot be an *idealist* construal. Also there needs to be awareness of norms; thus an *empiricist* picture-theory of knowledge is also inadequate. Vollenhoven defends a *critical (or transcendental) realism*, whereby subject and object each has its relevant, determining role.

Intuition, in turn, introduces the importance of conviction. Intuition is predicated on a bi-unity of Self-and-intramental reality. Its heart is the concrete intuition (the conviction *that* I am affected *when* actually affected), and its off-shoots are the analytical intuition (recognizing similarity and difference) and the metaphysical intuition (surmising there is a reality behind the appearances). Intuition gives immediate awareness and insight.

Each of the three forms of intuition has a relevance for epistemology. The concrete intuition certifies the self-certainty of *self-consciousness*.

This is the (Cartesian) heart of conviction. The analytical intuition of similarity and difference allows one to grasp distinctive objective meaning, namely, the recognition of clearly-defined mental content. In this regard Vollenhoven makes use of Meinong's *theory of mental objects* (*Gegenstandstheorie*).[32] Thirdly, the metaphysical intuition is the upbeat for postulating the *principle of substance*. Here essence is taken to be the unchanging identity that controls the appearances of external objects in their changing properties, qualities, and development. The essence of a thing is its thing-law, also said to be the Idea of distinctive being. Each person (Self) and thing (non-Self) has its determining Idea.

What Vollenhoven, on reflection, comes to find particularly wanting in these views is the subject-object relation that both knowledge and intuition exemplify: knowledge as regards an external object, intuition with respect to the intra-mental objects. What is missing is the direct relevance of truth. In his revised Reformed epistemology truth is placed much more in the open. There is also a change as regards intuition, strictly so-called. The concrete intuition Vollenhoven finds to be too psychological to serve as the justifying basis of knowledge. A more relevant basis is the immediate identification of discerning. The term used for this is "*schouwen*," which has the connotation of seeing or viewing and not just undergoing.

2. *The props of theism*

But, to continue the discussion of the early view: the reality that the principle of metaphysics postulates is that of the Self and the World (non-Self). These are the mainstays of Vollenhoven's metaphysics. It is at this point that the topic of theism is introduced.

The Self (we said) needs to acknowledge the relevance of norms. These may be norms of logic (said to be norms of truth) or truth in the context of knowledge, but also norms of ethics for action, norms of aesthetics for art, norms of religion for the religious life, etc. The Self is not as such a subject. Only when abiding by norms does the Self gain the status or take on the mentality of "knowing subject" (similarly for "ethical subject," "religious subject," etc.). The things of the World, in turn, can be known only on the assumption that their changeability is not a bewildering chaos. Some control needs to be operative so that the changes in

---

32 It is customary to use the German rendition *Gegenstand* (plural *Gegenstände*) in English. The term is retained in the context of revised Reformed epistemology. The insistence on the self-identity of a term of meaning distinguishes a *Gegenstand* from a fleeting mental content that I just happen to be aware of at a certain moment in time. For more discussion, cf. Kok 1992: 169–186 and Tol 2010: 122–136.

things are compatible with their discerned constant identity. Thus things are assumed to have controlling thing-laws or Ideas that serve to warrant their identity.

We see a rough analogy here between the Self and the (things of) the World. When we wonder where the *norms* come from that the Self has to abide by to warrant its knowing, then the analogous question about the World also comes readily to mind: from whence the *Ideas* that control the changeability of things in their appearances? Both questions concern governance, the former regarding the knowing subject, the latter the knowable object. (Understanding governance has direct implication with regard to understanding the Self and the World, hence formally we are touching on a *logos*-structure here, though Vollenhoven does not use this term explicitly at this point.) Vollenhoven accounts for governance by securing each kind in a *form of divinity*.

Norms have their seat in the Holy Spirit, which is how their existence is maintained: "the Spirit posits and maintains the norms and ideals. . ." (1918a: 410). In stating that it is the Spirit who maintains the validity of norms for the human being, we need to realize that this is no threat to human freedom. The Self needs to *willingly* abide by norms, but it is existentially possible to ignore them and, in fully humanist fashion, proceed by its own lights. The Ideas, or thing-laws, in turn, are taken to be "thoughts of God [the Father]" (1918a: 346; 1921c: 86, n.4). Ideas are the means whereby the "Counsel of the Creator" maintains the things of the World. This is a predestining Counsel. There is a strict determinism here between the thing-laws and the appearances of the things controlled by these laws. The relevance of these two Persons of the Trinity comes close to defining the very perspective that Vollenhoven took "Christian philosophy" to include: "Christian philosophy is dualistic because, being normative [as ideal], it distinguishes moral freedom from natural necessity" (1918a: 3).[33]

3. *Subjective and objective rationality*
The acceptance of the presence of divinity is not merely a gratuitous addition that comes through the Christian believer's faith. The relevance of these Persons becomes more evident through their operation. Here we see a rationality at work that is relevant, on the one hand, to the Self and the Self's movement of thought through which it acquires knowledge and, on the other hand, to the essential nature of the World that one strives to know. But each type of governance operates in its own way.

---

33 For a fuller discussion cf. Tol 2010: 180–185.

As to the norms that govern the Self's movement as knowing subject, one must be aware that practical life is factual and hence as such not normative. It is determined by the will and by emotional pleasure and pain. But they are able to stand in the way of the demands of the norms, in which case the knowing subject must "eliminate" them; "thus the norm demands that the truth be acknowledged, separated from pleasure and pain, *sine ira et studio* [without positive and negative prejudice], even if the *factually* existent Self as subject of willing does not want this" (1918a: 430; cf. also Tol 2010: 154–156). On the positive side there is the demand that the Self, as knowing subject, "avails itself of a healthy psycho-physical organization," involving at least "a maximum of keen sense-organs and of memory" (idem.).

What are we to make of this? The demand of norms – as fed by the Holy Spirit – foists on the Self an impossible dilemma: how can the Self eliminate a part of itself against its own will? This impossible situation is somewhat tempered by the assumption that there is a deep chasm between the factual side of human experience and the normed side of the knowing subject. There is a contrast in the human being that can call up a *tension*, which, in turn, puts the Self at odds with itself. At the same time we see that for the knowing subject to function properly it needs to be able to count on the "elimination" of the factual elements that might impede its own operation. The point of it all seems to be to stimulate "psychic growth," whereby the achievement of a real advance in knowing justifies whatever "elimination" is required on the factual side (1918a: 413; Tol 2010: 101). Thus we may speak here of a "subjective order," a total attitude as regards knowledge acquisition. This order specifies (I believe) what is needed to be *rational*: (i) the proper functioning of psycho-physical factors, (ii) elimination of what impedes knowledge acquisition, and (iii) abidance by the norms that consolidate the attitude of being a knowing subject. The anthropology supporting this view has a deep discontinuity between body and soul. The soul has truck with the *sacred*, when norms of the Spirit are respected, while the body is a dubious partner with a penchant for factual, *secular*, waywardness.[34]

A broadly similar situation holds in connection with the World. We

---

34 This is of course a scholastic anthropology of the Self as "*substantia completa*," and its body and soul as "*substantiae incompletae*"; each is incomplete as regards the whole Self. There is a common factor of psychical reality, namely in the psycho-physical organization of the body and the soul's psychical turning towards norms. Through this psychical factor body and soul "attach" to the Self; it is also through this factor that the Self controls the bi-unity of soul and body in psychical growth. See also the observation in footnote 18 above.

have already indicated how the Ideas (of distinct being) are substances that control the functioning properties, qualities, and development of individual things. In the Creator's predestining Counsel these Ideas are organized in a way that determines the course of the World through time. The foundation of this arrangement, as humanly understood, lies in the distinction between essence (or substance) and appearances. This is a distinction that also imposes a deep riff in our understanding of the world. The appearances are outer, visible, and fleeting, while essence is inner, invisible, and unchanging. Things are a duality, consisting of a hidden determining factor and a revealed outer compliance. What keeps these together? The young Vollenhoven does not (to my knowledge at least) say so explicitly, but a very likely candidate is "pre-established harmony."[35] This is a cosmic condition or principle that the Creator would appear to abide by in his predestining determination of the whole course of things. The addition of this principle to the essence-appearance assumption conditions the understanding of the World in a way that makes it all comprehensible. This constitutes a model of objective rationality. Here too, essence partakes of the *sacred* (God's Counsel), appearance of the *secular* (the World).[36]

So for both the Self and the World the distinction of the sacred and the secular fits snugly over the deep contrasting tension one finds between the main parts of both the Self and the World. No doubt this is intentional, for it gives extra point to the appeal to divinity. But at the same time this induces adherence to the *logos* of scholasticism that favors such an arrangement. Is this really the only way – and thus by default the correct way – to understand the human being and the World? Each is presented here as having bodily and material components in its makeup that are inherently wayward, "bad," and offset by components of mind and spirit that are more favored by divinity, hence "good." The moral difference of good and bad would appear to be inherent traits of creation, but at the same time one senses an incompatibility with the "(very) good

---

35   This "guess" commends itself in that Vollenhoven, in his dissertation, sees the world from a monadological perspective. Leibniz is of influence here. Though Vollenhoven criticizes him for not holding to "Platonic Ideas," Leibniz's principle of pre-established harmony – "predestination" being its theological counterpart – makes sense in Vollenhoven's context here.

36   There is also a problem cutting across the Self-World distinction. The human body is part of the material order, hence falls under the determinism that governs that order. It then appears to be futile to emphasize a responsibility towards encouraging proper functioning and eliminating unwelcome expressions, since there is no (or at least very little) freedom at this level to make this relevant in the face of determinism.

creation" proclaimed in Scripture. When Vollenhoven came to take serious stock of this situation – no doubt as part of the revised understanding of Calvinism referred to earlier (note 11) – he came to hold, as properly Reformed, that good and bad are *directions* of existential-historical activity, which affect mind and body alike. This revised view calls for a *logos* of creation that is integral, offering no opportunity to secure a fundamental contrast or opposition in the make-up of the created human being and the cosmos.

4. *The Logos and the theistic ideal*

The appeal to divinity has so far left out of account the second Person of the Trinity, the Son or divine Logos.[37] This was not due to irrelevance, rather it is to allow for an additional facet of knowledge that still needs to be mentioned, a facet relevant to making judgments and forming concepts. That facet is reconciliation. The early Vollenhoven strives to mediate any dualism or polarity and turn this into a reconciled bi-unity. This is realized by bringing in a "third element" between subject and object, an element that acts as a relation, binding the opposites together. The intuition is ideally suited to help carry this out. For it has of itself already the form of a bi-unity, namely of something immediately grasped by the Self. Intuition also has the role of *qualifying* the scholasticism the early Vollenhoven defends in terms of intuition's more human capacity to convince.

Achieving bi-unity is of the essence of knowledge. When knowledge is established, that means that there is achieved reconciliation of thought and being. Every properly formed judgment, in its primary structure of subject (of judgment) and predicate, signals this achievement. The subject of a judgment is an entity (whether a person or a thing) selected from the thought-alien side of the World. Something of its appearance is "picked up" (through forms of sensibility) and is now assimilated in a form of thought to become a predicate (*Gegenstandstheorie* helps make this clear and distinct.) When the predicate is attributed to the selected referent entity, then the synthesis of judgment takes place. (If we furthermore take all the predicates of a referent entity together we form a

---

37 Cf. also Tol 2010: 185–201. The uses of "Logos" and "*logos*" need to be kept apart. The first, in referring to the second Person of the Trinity, is an accepted English term (hence capitalized and not italicized); the second a foreign term (Greek, hence italicized and not capitalized) related to intelligence. The meaning of the second gets to overlap with that of the first when speculative notions of Christology are advocated. Vollenhoven never hesitated to use the term "Logos" in reference to the Christ, as in the Gospel of John. As to the use of "*logos*," when the terms "logical law-sphere" and "modal order" came into use, the term "*logos*" became redundant.

concept of the entity. A concept can never be completely adequate to the entity in question, but it can be in step with the ideal of the growth of our understanding. Judgment therefore is prior to concept formation.)

This view of knowledge, as achieved synthesis, has it that knowledge is at once a relation between the Self and the World and a reality in its own right (as a moment of realized reconciliation). This needs a warrant to keep it in proper perspective. To that end the divine Logos, the Son, is introduced. What exactly is his role? (The following diagram gives an overview of theism at this point, taken from Tol 2010: 201.)

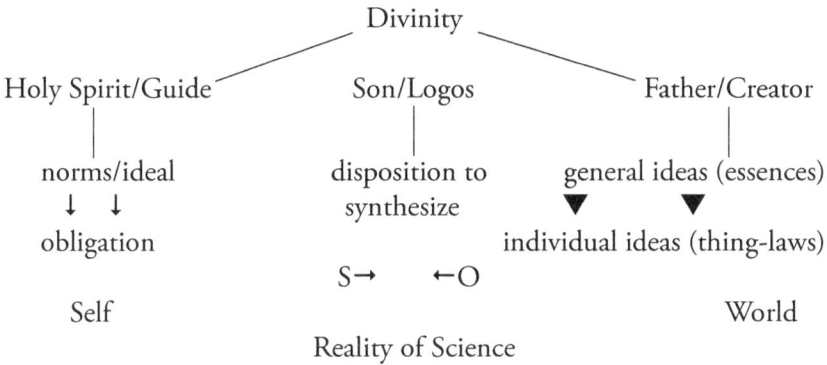

<pre>
                          Divinity
                      /   \
Holy Spirit/Guide   Son/Logos   Father/Creator
        | | |
   norms/ideal   disposition to   general ideas (essences)
     ↓   ↓   synthesize   ▼   ▼
   obligation   individual ideas (thing-laws)
                           S→   ←O
      Self   World
                      Reality of Science
</pre>

['↓': impinge upon; '▼': individuation]
["S": subject of knowing; "O": object known]

In the first place, the interaction of the Self and the World that is prior to the synthesis is not an automatic process. There needs to be an *operating motive* that will 'trigger the synthesis. Vollenhoven attributes to the Logos the "disposition . . . of subject and object of knowledge . . . to enter into a synthesis" (1918a: 410). If we were to ignore this and view such a disposition from an immanent perspective, one of two likely alternatives would immediately appear. (i) There is the idealist variety, in which the Self interprets knowledge as a means of dominating over the World. After all, the World is thought-alien, so human control over it seems fitting. (ii) Then there is the materialist variety, which sees knowledge as enhancing a naturalistic process. This seeks to make responsibility and accountability on the side of the Self redundant. Neither of these varieties, of speculative idealism and naïve empiricism respectively, discloses in knowledge the possibility of its own unique dimension. When viewed from the perspective of the Logos – that of realized reconciliation – getting to know the world is enriching for the Self at the same time that it increases the Self's responsibility for the World. This view has definite merit over against the two alternative views.

Secondly, the interaction of Self and World that takes place in the knowledge process calls into play the forms of rationality that are ensconced in the Self and the World. It is part and parcel of classical Scholasticism to look on the relevance of the subjective and objective orders of rationality as being in harmony. One appeals to the Logos to certify this by taking it to be the *source of rationality*. Thus the order that marks subjective psychical growth in the individual cannot be at odds with the objective pre-established harmony of the world in light of a common transcendent rationality. And since the Logos is the Christ of Christian belief, the Christian faith would appear to be relevant as safeguard of any use of rationality in its role of mediating knowledge growth. The unfortunate side of this view is that rationality is taken to be an epistemic fixed trait rather than an ideal that one ought to pursue in a properly responsible manner, not to speak of the intellectualization of faith assumed here for faith to be at all able to offer this security of thought.

In the third place, in consequence of the harmony of the two orders, the Logos is also the assurance that the ideal of a complete understanding (= the knowing subject's adequate concept) represents a *complete knowledge of the Idea* of the World. It is in this sense that Vollenhoven speaks specifically of *theism as ideal*. The theistic ideal concerns "the epistemic system that God wants that we form concerning all the given" (1918a: 443). In realizing this ideal, knowledge is honored as positing its own reality. This is especially important for, and made more tangible through, the philosophy of science. For scientific knowledge anticipates this epistemic system in pursuing the ideal. It does this via a *formal-material method*. The structure or formal side of this knowledge can be understood through the intuitionist formal insight of *Gegenstandstheorie*. The material side provides the data that constitute the facts of a science. In their bi-unity they delineate the "organism of science." The Self "works at" the insight, guided by the ideal; the World "reveals the facts," which can only be what they are. In the organism of science, neither the Self nor the World predominate, which is why Vollenhoven takes their bi-unity to be a scientific reality, a "third reality" beside that of the Self and the World (cf. Vollenhoven 1918a: 96, 106, 381, 434–437; also Tol 2010: 190–197). The ideal of a complete knowledge can never be factually achieved. But that does not make reconciliation and its meliorative growth redundant. Growth in knowledge is itself a real benefit. "Theism grows through the psychical synthesis of the *sôma Xristou* [the body of

Christ] and is only complete at the end of the ages" (1918a: 443). Christ the Logos upholds the ideal meaning of the reality of science that the body of Christ, namely the Christian community, consciously implements and works at. In the meantime, the faith-community – the "body of Christ" in its primary meaning – is at the same time the most promising intellectual community in light of the ideal of complete knowledge of the Idea to which it would appear to have access.

Theism as ideal seeks to secure intelligibility and rational use in divinity. A theist is not merely a philosopher who confesses to believing in God. After all, that person may wish to keep the world of thought and the world of faith quite separate. Such a philosopher has no theistic ideal. However a philosopher who is prone to defend this ideal, as philosophically relevant, has the tradition of scholasticism to fall back on. This offers a variety of models from the history of philosophy in which rationality is itself thought to have certainty through its divine origin. The early Vollenhoven made his own choices in this regard. If we take reason to be rationality in use, then reason in the early Vollenhoven is not merely the use of rationality that is sanctioned by the Logos, it is also a use applied by the Self in the context of the World, each of which has sacred and secular features, as governed by distinct forms of divine activity. Though one may and should raise serious questions in this regard, it is to Vollenhoven's merit that, while emphasizing that divine activity evinces the operation of a "Divine Reasonableness" (1918a: 444), the latter is an operation that is *distinct* from human reason, to which human reason cannot measure up. Thus the human adherence to the theistic ideal entails being aware of limitations. In other words, the early Vollenhoven did not propose "thinking God's thought after him" (as in Augustine), which evinces no consciousness of limitations.

Nevertheless, Vollenhoven came to the assessment that the scholastic feature of his position hindered the proper understanding of the boundaries that knowledge and science call for. In that light, the term "theistic ideal" is too "scholastically loaded" to be maintained in a revised context. The revision he proposed held that, in epistemology and science, a Reformed philosopher's faith entails being called to fulfill a God-given *task* (§§77, 183; also 1926b: 381–382), a "high but limited task of science" (§210). The term "task" entails an "office of responsibility." Being a "knowing agent" involves "task consciousness" (1926b: 382, 396; 1926d: 61). He took this to be part and parcel of the religious office of the believer's being a "prophet" (1926d: 55). This is quite other than discovering in oneself a fund of rationality. A Reformed philosopher is a believer who senses that being rational is not to avail over something ready to hand or intrinsic to mind (as justified by faith), but that rationality comes to prevalence only through the proper response (in executing an office of responsibility) to intuited creaturely conditions and norms.

5. *The Reformed principles*

In defending the subjective order and the objective order in epistemology, the young Vollenhoven was in step with the university's concern about "Reformed principles." As stated in their report about these principles, Woltjer and Kuyper had written: "under '[Reformed] principles' is *not* to be understood those starting points which lie in the facts and in the essence of things, but such principles as, in consciousness, control the world of thought" (Woltjer and Kuyper 1895: 8; cf. also Tol 2010: 47–50). This acknowledges the two orders of thought and being that the early Vollenhoven had worked with. In concentrating on the "world of thought" – since this is "in consciousness," the Self is its locus – the starting points in the facts and the essence of things are not reckoned to be unimportant, rather they can "function in the foundation of education only after being expressed in the form of thoughts" (ibid.). In other words, the thoughts on the side of human consciousness need to be developed so as to become (progressively more) adequate to grasping the starting points in the World. (This is the essence of the "theistic ideal" as Vollenhoven had it; cf. above.) The Reformed principles are meant to guide the development of human consciousness and knowledge acquisition so as to attain a more "adequate concept" of the objective starting points in facts and essences of the World. The arrangement here is scholasticism in a nutshell.

The writers of the report aver that it has been given to Calvinism, itself a "higher life form" granted by God within Christianity (Woltjer and Kuyper 1895: 9), to implement this intellectual project. The Reformed principles lie in the region that Vollenhoven referred to as norms guiding the Self as subject (in its various forms). It then comes as no surprise that the report expresses interest in Kant and the knowing subject at this point (ibid: 13). This modern development of epistemology outside of Calvinism also focuses on the Self, in fact takes it as its point of departure, and thus, despite its humanism in this Kantian setting, it nevertheless has the potential of possibly being of service in helping Calvinism to execute its program of a Reformed epistemology, provided that it holds firmly to its own scholastic setting (ibid: 14; cf. also §212).

H. *The revised Reformed epistemology in outline*

Vollenhoven's discussion of epistemology in his inaugural address has the negative aim of self-consciously guarding against a relapse into humanism and scholasticism. This negative facet is developed in the historical part of his address. He intersperses his discussion with remarks about his own view, which we now know is a *revised* view as compared to his initial theism. His remarks here remain fragmentary, in the knowledge that other work, just published or being published (namely, 1926b and 1926d), provides a more connected account. It goes too far to attempt to pull it all together here.[38] Some things have already come up for discussion. We will now attempt to indicate the epistemological essentials more by way of an overview.[39]

The epistemology Vollenhoven here espouses is essentially three-layered. Most basic is the *intuition*. Here is the starting point of all knowing. It starts with *discerning*. Then there is *knowledge*. At this point language, communication, and judgments are relevant. The third layer is *thought*. Thought may disclose and renew or criticize and correct against the background of what we know. Thought is also central to concept formation. The factor that runs through these three layers is truth, taken realistically. It has its seat in the intuition of discerning. It is central to knowledge, for the essence of knowledge is said to be "possessing truth." And in connection with thought, or more particularly in concept formation, the latter is described as "truth grasped in a form." On each a word.

1. *Intuition.*

Vollenhoven's initial understanding of intuition, as rooted in self-consciousness, was short-lived. Knowing that one is affected when undergoing an experience – the prime feature of the "concrete intuition" – no longer suits Vollenhoven's purposes for two reasons. In the first place it expresses the certainty of possessing something inwardly rather than being more secured by what that something is (§§22, 46). In other words, it is difficult to distinguish this intuition from inner perception, and that goes to show that it is more psychological than cognitive. In the second place, the yield of this inner intuition is unitary representations of content or of acts. If they are to serve as the basis of knowledge, then they have to be brought together in such a way that a truth results. But where

---

38 For more detailed discussions cf. Kok 1992, chapter 7: "Logos, states of affairs and knowledge"; also parts of Tol 2010, chapter 4, are relevant.

39 In delving into epistemology at this point we leave out of account the relevance of the forms of divinity for Vollenhoven's *revised* Reformed position. The discussion is opened in Tol 2010, chapter 4, IIIB: "The boundary threefold"; pp. 422–454.

does truth, which is not a psychological trait, come from? The humanist answer points to the creativity of the human mind, in its synthesizing role. But for a level-headed Calvinist this is more than a questionable anthropology.

The intuition Vollenhoven now defends is one that accords with the presuppositions of the Reformed position (see section C above). Human beings, as living creatures, are always already in the world realizing a life-attitude, and they are practically involved in all the capacities a human being has at his disposal. Primary – in an epistemological sense – is the *discerning* of the kinds of activities relevant to our *Sitz im Leben*. Here the principle of sphere sovereignty is relevant as leading indication, namely in addressing the basic awareness of living in a pluralist world and having to discharge one's duties in diversely determined ways. (There is some-thing of the primitive features of *conscience* here.)

Such discerning is an intuitive *viewing* of differences in *practical be-ing*. What one discerns are "modes of being," suited to the characteristic qualities of the different kinds of practice. The term *modality* is put to effect here, as denoting the most encompassing "adverbial" quality of a discerned kind of practice. When formulated in judgments, Vollenhoven speaks of "judgments of discerning or of existence" (§§15, 86). Discern-ing [*ontwaring*] is distinguished from perceiving [*waarnemen*] (§§20, 82, 86). The schema of a judgment of discerning is "A is" (§§36, 199).[40]

The doctrine of sphere sovereignty provides an interpretation in terms of "law-spheres." A law-sphere is a modally distinct sphere of prac-tice, namely, of conduct that is rule-bound. One accepts, as primary da-tum of experience, that there is a diversity in kinds of practice and thus a diversity of law-spheres.[41] Human beings participate directly in all the law-spheres, irrespective of whether they are relevant to nature or culture. Non-human creatures, being (much) more limited in their participation in kinds of activity, are limited to the law-spheres relevant solely to the natural world. The "intersection principle," which states that each in-dividual creature – for Vollenhoven an "essence" – is intersected by a diversity of law-spheres, makes the participation of creatures an essential trait of their being.[42]

---

40 This is perhaps unnecessarily elliptic. Presumably Vollenhoven means to say "A is such and such," for the being that is referred to by "is" includes modality. Then the intuition on which a judgment of discerning is based could be indicated as "A's such-ness" (understood as "A's primary or primitive such-ness").

41 The necessity of distinguishing a diversity of law-spheres finds support in the prin-ciple that antinomies are to be excluded; cf. Tol 2010: 400–404.

42 This is not said to be a principle, but, in being so primary, it does serve as one, which

Now it is against this background that knowledge and thought, in turn, are related to being. Their possibility also has an intuitionist trait. The intersection principle provides for the possibility of primary knowledge of being. In this sense we find "knowing resorting under being" as attested by judgments of discerning.[43] But knowledge is more than what judgments of discerning provide, however basic their contribution is. When our knowing is formulated in judgments one realizes that the "is" of judgment, whereby a predicate is attributed to a subject of judgment, involves determination. This, in turn calls for intelligence, at least intelligence of the sort that allows determination to make sense.[44] Viewed from Vollenhoven's standpoint, the feature of intelligence called for is the logical law-sphere, the warrant of creaturely intelligibility, and its analogical reflection in every non-logical law-sphere, as known modally. In other words, this is the *logos* as interwoven in the vertical dimension of being. Thus one needs to be able to bring a distinct law-sphere (in terms of its modality) into focus to appreciate its determination of intelligibility, in which the logical analogy of the modality concerned plays a vital and distinct role. Each law-sphere offers a different kind of epistemic determination, which, when acknowledged as to its modality, is what Vollenhoven calls a "*gezichtsveld*"—literally: "field of view", here translated as "circle of consideration."[45] We say more about knowledge immediately below.

Thought too has an intuitive feature. It presupposes a viewed circle of consideration. Thought involves the use of both the logical modality and the logical analogy in the non-logical law-spheres (as viewed circles of consideration). The logical modality provides the logical schema of relatedness, i.e., a system of relation and terms. The thinking subject puts this schema to work by focusing it (in a horizontal sense) on the logical analogy present in a viewed, hence chosen, (non-logical) circle of consid-

---

is why judgments about the intersection of an individual essence are said to be metaphysical; cf. §§20, 120, 128. Intersection also figures in the background of "circle of consideration" (§§67, 126) and "field of inquiry" (§32), these being specialized applications of "law-sphere" (see below).

43   Nothing is explicitly said of this in the current text. For "knowing's resorting under being" see Vollenhoven 2005d/e: §§8, 23, 147. This would appear to be the "discovery" made about mid-1922. If so, it evidences Vollenhoven's move away from adhering to the distinction of thought and being as fundamental distinction. Cf. also Tol 2010: 364–368.

44   The topic of determination is not made explicit in *Logos and Ratio*. One finds it discussed in the early lecture notes: 26msA and 27msA.

45   See §66; the term "circle of consideration" is chosen, for lack of a better one. In Tol 2010: 330, n.173, I opted (with apology) for the more literal "field of vision"; John Kok, in Kok 1992: 248 ff., chose for "intellectual horizon."

eration. In this way the thinking subject illuminates relational features in the logical analogy, which now gets to be represented in the logical modality as logical content or relational *states of affairs* (§144). How this logical content (or states of affairs) gets to *represent* the relational features in a circle of consideration remains a mystery (1926b: 397). Yet it is in virtue of representation that one claims there is a "something" to think about truly. This is the basic intuition of thought. In fact the scope of this "something," relevant to a circle of consideration, determines a "field of inquiry" (*gedachteveld*) (§§66, 67, 166).

2. *Knowledge*

The central theme in epistemology is knowledge, and knowledge is generally taken to be represented by judgments (and concepts, but they will be discussed under the next heading). Judgments have a subject-predicate structure, usually described as a synthesis of the subject-term and the predicate-term. These terms derive from experience, from which knowledge arises. Vollenhoven agrees with the subject-predicate form of a judgment, but he cannot accept this as being of the essence of knowledge. The use of judgments presupposes a more primary (and not necessarily verbalized) insight. It is the *state* of having insight that is described as "possessing truth," and when being in that state truth effectuates its own security.

Truth is here understood in the realist sense of being truth "as such." Admittedly it is difficult to grasp this, especially when truth is said to be truth through "nothing but its own character" (§66). Vollenhoven thereby emphasizes that truth is not truth by virtue of any dependence on something else, such as being possessed by the mind. It isn't the certainty of having it mentally that counts, though naturally we can delude ourselves in thinking we possess a certain truth. To look for guards against delusion is again to turn the problem of knowledge into one of psychology. It is better to look for what truth actually secures.

Truth does have a context, not for its own definition but for its own operation. If knowledge is truth possessed, then clearly there must be a *knowing agent* who possesses it, but there must also be something that the truth is about. Truth must represent something, about which the truth gives knowledge to the agent. This something is the *knowable referent*. The appearing together of knowing agent and knowable referent assumes the relevance of a specific circle of consideration that modally modifies the knowing. Hence the situation of knowledge is not captured by the twofold "subject-object schema," but the *threefold*: "knowing agent –

truth – knowable referent."

The effect of truth is that it serves to put the knowing agent in a satisfying relation to the knowable referent, something not to be expected when deluded, for error spells waywardness.[46] If I possess the truth of knowing my way home, then I am able to get home (other things being equal). This is not just relevant as a case of "knowing how," it holds of other forms of knowing too, e.g., such as "knowing that." My claim that I know that 2+3=5 or that metal expands when heated can be immediately challenged, calling for a demonstration to verify my insight, or at least to put to good effect what I (claim to) know.[47] But in each case the insight – the truth as such – is primary and prior to any use, demonstration, or practical application. This includes its becoming the content of a judgment.

A judgment puts a truth, when once turned into the content of a judgment, into a more workable form. This calls for the application of language. Through language use, a truth can be verbalized when formulated in a subject-predicate schema. But truth as such and the truth of a judgment are not the same (1926b: 384).[48] There is a difference in how truth is "handled." One needs to reflect (on earlier intuitions) and make choices (in connection with relevant concepts) when coming to "pronounce" a judgment ("*vellen van een oordeel*"; §§25, 42, 115). The latter is an active moment, the endpoint of a process, while truth as such "rests" (1926b: 384). Most would agree that a formulated insight seldom does complete justice to the insight as such. This raises the question as to a relevant relation between knowledge and language.

In this connection Vollenhoven asks how a truth comes to be pos-

---

46   This "effect of truth" should not be confused with pragmatism. For the latter the "satisfying relation" *defines* truth (James 1992: 44) as suits its empiricism. Vollenhoven presupposes, as properly discerned, an intuition of modality that is lacking in pragmatism. If, in a specific case, the intuition of modality is gotten wrong or is entirely missing, then the hoped for satisfaction is very likely to prove to be ephemeral.

47   Vollenhoven emphasizes the difference between two kinds of knowing: "knowing of" and "knowing that" (cf. §§22, 26, 59, 192). The former is in Vollenhoven's view relevant to psychology, not cognition. When limited to a psychological understanding, then the subject-object relation suffices and one can speak of "knowledge of." However cognition calls for the distinct factor of truth. Cf. Vollenhoven 1926d: 54–55.

48   In 1926b: 385 Vollenhoven states: "Truth – I mean the non-verbalized and what is prior to becoming the possession of the knowing agent – *can* appear as possession of the knowing agent and as content of a judgment. But neither context is essential for the essence of truth."

sessed by a knowing agent. He distinguishes two ways: it can be *conveyed* to the knowing agent or it can be *sought* by the agent (1926b: 382–383). When conveyed, the vehicle of conveyance is language. Someone communicates truth/information to someone else. The sender most often communicates through verbalization, which usually involves formulating judgments. If the recipient takes the communication seriously – he believes that the sender is trustworthy and that he isn't being fooled, etc. – then he will subsequently try to get at the truth by focusing on the content of the judgments involved. He "unpacks" the judgments and thereby comes to see the truth that is meant. Very much of our knowledge is actually acquired in this way as knowledge by communication. It plays a key role in religious revelation, but also much of our learning takes place through what we hear or read and what is taught to us (1926b: 385). (That doesn't mean we always give adequate attention to the last step of getting at the insight as such. Too often we take the medium for the message.)

When, on the other hand, truth is sought there are not, as yet, concomitant judgments available. One first needs to get at the truth by inquiry – assuming an adequate context of discovery – and only when the truth as such is found will it be formulated in judgment form. The verbalization puts the truth in a more usable form for purposes of organization and argument (cf. 1926d: 58). This is of special importance in a scientific context, as indeed is also suggested by the alternative of truth being sought by inquiry. This involves the topic of thought, to which we turn presently.

Other features related to knowledge occur in Vollenhoven at this point, e.g., the topics of nominalism (§§42–43), faith and knowledge (§§75–76), and the distinct role of representations (§§17, 30, 33, 123; 1926d: 149). We leave these for the reader to explore. The features that we have discussed are particularly relevant to Vollenhoven's revised work. In that sense the revision evidences his self-criticism. Most prominent in this respect is the theme of truth. But the bottom line is Vollenhoven's attempt to bring epistemology under the sway of the newly interpreted Reformed standpoint.

3. *Thought*

Thought and knowledge, or thinking and knowing, form an important distinction. Here "thought" is not meant, Cartesian-wise, as synonym for "consciousness." That would put it in the forefront of any discerning or distinction. In fact that was Vollenhoven's earlier use, when he proceeded from the distinction of thought and being. He now considers thought in a more restrictive sense, against the background of knowledge. In this position either it can serve to discover truth, in which case it adds to our fund of knowledge, or it may refine our knowledge, i.e., correct (what we took to be) knowledge (1926d: 150). But thought is not a mere appendix of knowing. It has its own focus. Whereas knowing, in line with its roots in intuition, aims to possess truth directly, thinking on the other hand approaches truth more mediately, by grasping it via the use of a "form." Vollenhoven sees this as typical for *concept formation*. To effectuate this, the human being is required to be logically active, as we found, in the act of bringing together "form and content." While knowing is a *state* of being-in-the-know, thinking *effects* a synthesis of conceptual understanding (§§131, 144). This synthesis is also important for the methodical procedures of a science (as we will briefly point out below; cf. Vollenhoven 1926d: 59).

The operating base of concept formation is a "field of inquiry" (*gedachtenveld*). Given the background of thought in knowing, a field of inquiry presupposes a viewed circle of consideration. The intersection principle is relevant here too, enabling "things" (individuals or essences) to be known in terms of relevant circles of consideration. Now while "things" are here meant in their full scope, it is also possible to view only the specific intersect of a distinct circle of consideration. The "thing" is then relevant only as truncated by the limited view (§67) – say, as considered spatially, or organically or economically, etc.[49] This obviously involves conscious activity on the part of the agent, who, having truncated things to one discerned circle of consideration, is analytically busy. (Technically, this involves being specifically focused on the logical analogy of the circle of consideration in question, which is how a circle of consideration is turned into a field of inquiry; §66.) In other words, the *agent* is now a "thinking agent," a Self ensconced in the logical law-sphere, hence subject to logical norms, but an agent that is also provided with a "logical instrument" with which to think rationally. That instrument is the logical schema of relatedness, i.e., the system of terms-in-relation. The *referent*, in turn, is not just the knowable referent. It is now an "object of thought" to the extent that the referent has relational relevance and is represented

---

49   The "individual thing" that is intersected by a viewed circle of consideration remains unitary, as when assessing the relevance of predication, (say) "Bill is ill." But when analysed systemically, the person is reduced to the organic level of a life system in being confronted by the logical schema of relatedness. Bill's relevance is then no longer unitary, he now being relevant merely as a case of a specific life system in the biological field of inquiry.

in the logical law-sphere as logical content, what Vollenhoven calls "states of affairs." The latter is not the truncated (a-logical) "something" in the circle of consideration, as viewed by the thinking agent, but states of affairs *represent* that something *in* the logos or logical law-sphere. (As stated earlier, the reality of what is represented simply has to be accepted as basic—"by virtue of creation"; §§66, 137; 1926b: 397–398). Hence a science's "field of inquiry" is an area in the *logos* populated by states of affairs.

Concept formation takes place in a field of inquiry. This formation is a synthesis, a merging of the logical schema with relevant states of affairs. The "merging" attests to our understanding, and this involves giving form content. The form of the logical schema takes on a specific shape in confrontation with specific states of affairs. (Vollenhoven once spoke of the thinking agent "scooping up" content by means of the logical schema as shovel; §155.) In less picturesque language, the states of affairs encumber the logical schema or form. The states of affairs themselves are present in terms of three categories: (i) there are "objects" or "terms" – Vollenhoven prefers to use the German tern "*Gegenstände*" – which represent referable things; (ii) there is the "essential connection," which represents the main connections between referable things; and (iii) there is the modality that represents the relevant circle of consideration of the referable things and their connections. It is only as categories of representation that the representations are logical; that which is represented is of a non-logical nature. But it is only in the guise of representations that the thinking agent gets to understand his material rationally. This logical content has to fit the logical form, thus any case or example of relationship has to be able to encumber the logical form, as long as the encumbered content does not contravene the logical schema's relevance (1926b: 397). The systemic form of the logical schema gets to be modulated by the modality of the state of affairs, the relation of the schema is modulated by the "essential connection" in the state of affairs, and the terms (or "moments") are modulated by the *Gegenstände* of the states of affairs. (The latter represent the truncated material of the relevant circle of consideration.) This "modulation" takes place by thought and within the *logos*. Here we are getting at the essence of rationality. The latter is "the logical schema in use" as used by the thinking subject. The use is to select and grasp relational facets of states of affairs, and in encumbering the logical schema with the latter, there is (some measure of) synthesis in grasping the truth of the fit between form and content. The product of the synthesis is the concept of scientific (or logical) understanding. The merge or encumbrance is a way of grasping truth cognitively or rationally.

The importance of encumbering lies not only in being able to acquire scientific understanding, it is also a way that truth is had: "truth grasped in a form" (§15). When discussing knowledge, we found that truth puts the knowing agent in a satisfactory state to a known referent. There is no need to distinguish between the logical schema and states of affairs at this point (1926b: 399). In concept formation this is different. The relation of knowing agent and known referent now includes the *logos* and what it brings to bear. In particular, the knowing agent avails itself of the logical schema, and the knowable referent sides with the states of affairs in being represented by the latter (1926b: 399). In restricting the relation of knowing agent and knowable referent to that of logical schema using states of affairs, truth too becomes restricted to its *cognitive* sense. Cognitive truth results through the synthesis of form and affair. In being a formulated synthesis, its grasp on truth is subject to degrees, namely in being more or less successful. Hence rationality, in characterizing the use of the logical form and the states of affairs, is not a self-evident understanding but is rather subject to being a duty, to be fulfilled with care.

If cognitive truth is synthesis that is formed, subject to degrees, then encumbrance too must take place in degrees, between total failure (say, "malformed": the state of affairs are not adequately grasped by the form) and full adequacy ("well-formed"; §137). This yields falsehood as well as truth, respectively.[50] When the combination of form and content is not yet completed, Vollenhoven speaks (not very convincingly) of "negation" (§§35, 166). Concepts have what in current terminology is called "truth-value," i.e., have the intrinsic possibility of being true or false (and possibly a valence in between, if that is what Vollenhoven's "negation" implies).[51] In any case, in connection with concepts, truth or falsehood is not an addition placed there in virtue of their being accepted (asserted) or rejected (denied), respectively (by the thinking agent). Concepts in fact are like *propositions*, as Vollenhoven's identification of Bolzano's "*Sät-*

---

50 Vollenhoven's use of "logical form" and "states of affairs" is much like that of the metaphor in philosophy of science, namely the conceptual "net" cast over the "facts." Only the facts actually "caught" in the net contribute to the understanding, the latter being dependent on how "course or fine" the net is. At one point Vollenhoven compares his "logical form" to a spade that scoops up soil (§155), though perhaps a fork might have been a more suited metaphor (in letting finer soil through – subsystems – depending on the fork's own grade of coarseness).

51 Vollenhoven's "negation" seems to reflect the situation of assumption or consideration, short of any actual assertion or denial, something he also welcomes in Bolzano (§165). Vollenhoven's discussion at this point is rather inchoate, and perhaps confused.

ze an sich" with his own "concepts" also seems to suggest (§165). Are Vollenhoven's "concepts" (as propositions in disguise?) also entities "as such"? Whatever the correct reading is here, Vollenhoven's realism does not preclude his taking the features of process and formation seriously in connection with concepts that are after all "synthesized" or formed. (This holds of judgments too for that matter, as when being involved in the process of coming to pronounce a judgment, the process of "coming-to-know"; 1926b: 384)

Within a field of inquiry there is also the possibility of refining a system in terms of subsystems. The terms or "moments" of a system – as such the "things" as represented by its reduction to just the modality of the circle of consideration involved – may, through analysis, give rise to a subsystem in their own right (cf. §§20, 67, 157, 189). An example of the peculiar set-up of systems and subsystems may be illustrated in biology. In the main system individuals occur, not as wholes but as reduced to their life-functions, which in turn can be treated as terms ("cases") in (say) an investigation of a contagious disease. The disease in question is then the system, the contagion is the relation, and the organic functioning of individuals constitutes the terms of this relation of contagion. But each individual's functioning can in turn be treated as a (sub)system, namely, there is the biotic state of the individual, consisting of organs interrelating in a way that is indicative of one's general health. A further step is possible when considering each specific organ as a system (rather: a sub-subsystem), with its own containing relation and terms. In this way any term of a relation, i.e., any part of a system belonging to a circle of consideration, can potentially become a (sub)system in its own right upon discovering its own more limited relation and more detailed relata.

As final point we mention that concept formation has an extension in the methodology of a science. A method needs to be appropriate to a field of inquiry. Vollenhoven defends a *pluralist* methodology, for any particular method cannot trespass the circle of consideration in which a special science has its field of inquiry (§§127, 189). But certain things are common to every method. One common feature concerns the two "directions of proceeding." Concept formation is based on relational structures, some of which are very broad and general, others more detailed and special. One may advance from either a general system and by analysis work towards forming concepts of more detailed parts, "from the whole to the moments" (§189) – or equally from main system to subsystems, as in the example of biology above. This is to proceed in the (so-called) "complicating" direction. One may also pursue the opposite route, in the "simplifying" direction, and form concepts of a more general order (§§137, 189). Each direction is important.[52] Concept formation begins with what is easiest to understand. This can then be taken either in the complicating direction, in which more and more details are exposed, thus refining our conceptual understanding, or in the simplifying direction, towards the foundation of the science in question.[53] Vollenhoven makes a special point of pinpointing the meaning of "general" and "special" in terms of these methodical directions (§§23, 66, 189). General concepts tend to occur in the more foundational part of scientific understanding and also recur more often than concepts introduced farther away from the foundations. Thus whether concepts are general or special needs to be ascertained by comparison in the context of their occurrence in the science as a whole. That whole is of course different for every circle of consideration.

4. *New developments*

In Vollenhoven's work of 1926, of which the inaugural address is an integral part, much is present that recurs in his later writings. In fact he has a quite remarkable grasp of his revised position over against his own earlier, more scholastic position. That scholastic position only began to give way in the course of 1922. His new interpretation of Calvinism remained constant in later years, as well as his emphasis on sphere sovereignty. The intuition operative in "knowing resorting under (practical) being" also remained a fixed attribute,[54] as did the distinction of the vertical and the horizontal dimensions (renamed in 1929 as "determinants"; cf. Vollenhoven 2005d/e). Some details of philosophical insight shifted, usually (at least the more important ones) in tandem with a deepening of concomitant historical insight.[55] One topic that becomes more prominent with time is the contrast of good and evil, as directions of the heart. Explicit statements on anthropology in the work of 1926 are conspicuously absent.[56]

---

52 They are later referred to in the more common terminology of "resolution" and "composition" respectively; see Tol 2010: 37-39.

53 This double direction methodology is precisely what Bertrand Russell specifies for mathematics in the opening chapter of Russell 1919: 1-2.

54 For example, Vollenhoven 1948: 16, Vollenhoven speaks of "the noetic" (*het gnotische*), meaning knowing and learning to know as taking place in practical life. The intuitionism remains implicit here.

55 For a more detailed indication, see the general introduction to Vollenhoven 2010, p. 55, note 56.

56 In the current text the use of "the soul" (§33) is as synonym for "the whole personality" (§115), said to be relevant in both knowing and perceiving. No further details are given. The expression "God's power holds body and soul together" (§120) is,

The philosophical picture sketched in the address is sometimes left very rough; e.g., while higher law-spheres are mentioned, such as the ethical (§184), juridical and economic life (§183), there is no attempt to be complete or to give the proper sequence of their listing. At other times matters were found to need adjusting. E.g., the modality of time (§124) was soon simply deleted. Vollenhoven, and H. Dooyeweerd too for that matter, came to defend a broader understanding of time.[57] Vollenhoven's distinction between kinematics and dynamics collapsed at the end of 1930, in favor of a unified "physical law-sphere,"[58] only to be resurrected again in the early 1950s by Dooyeweerd, with Vollenhoven's concurrence.[59]

By far the most far-reaching change, introduced early 1927, involved the position of the logical law-sphere. In the current text much depends on its being taken to be the first or lowest law-sphere in the "pyramid of the law-spheres" (§209). In consequence of that position every other law-sphere has the analogy of the logical in its make-up, which is essential for concept formation. Nevertheless, its position was moved to about midway the "modal pyramid," between the psychical and the historical-formative law-spheres.

The reason for the change was, to my knowledge, never made explicit in print (though lecture notes of the early years – 26msA and 27ms – discuss some of these matters, which cannot be addressed here). However, one may surmise a more anthropocentric concern at work. The initial bottom-sphere position of the logical was especially mindful of philosophy of science (or meta-logical) reasoning. The differences in method of the (main) sciences are accounted for in terms of the analogies relevant to a science's method. Because analogies are rooted in the cosmic order, the arrangement of the sciences is indicative of the cosmic order needed

I believe, a concession to Descartes, in using the latter's frame of reference at this point, for Vollenhoven rephrases this in his own terminology as "preservation of a cosmic unity [i.e., an individual]" despite its being "intersected by different law-spheres." However, the meanings of "body" and "soul" are not made explicit in this reformulation.

57 For an exploratory discussion of that understanding in Vollenhoven, see Tol 1995.

58 H. van Riessen retained something of the early position by defending the limited view of time as change, and taking change to be the essential connection of the physical law-sphere; Van Riessen 1959: 81, 82.

59 The changes and the developments of Reformed philosophy were often points of discussion between Vollenhoven and Dooyeweerd. They weren't always in agreement. Differences arose already in the mid-1920s. For Vollenhoven's view of these differences, cf. Tol and Bril 1992: 107ff, 184ff, 199ff. Their diverging paths are extensively discussed in Tol 2010: 275–380 and summarized in Tol 2011a.

to support them. The law-sphere that provides the "logical form" is then expected to be in first place. Its shift to a more mid-way position is based on more anthropological-functional reasoning, whereby the *function* of thought requires support in psychical awareness, which in turn rests on the organic-vital function of life, which is supported by physical-chemical systems, etc.

But the shift also created problems. There is now no longer a logical analogy in the law-spheres below the newly situated logical – now called "analytical" – modality. For analogies of a law-sphere occur in a higher sphere, not the other way around: "there is nothing of the latter spheres [i.e., those above the logical sphere] in the former [i.e., the logical sphere]" (§202). But that cannot mean that relational patterns are no longer relevant in the sub-analytical spheres.

It would appear that this situation was remedied in 1930(d) in a complex development that included at least the following items (briefly indicated).[60] In the first place, in the "vertical dimension" a modal-functional order is introduced of actual or "subject-functions" within individuals.[61] Like the original analogies, there is, in subject-functions, an analogical presence of the likeness of lower functions in a higher function, referred to as "retrocipations"; likewise – and this is novel – there is an analogical presence or likeness of higher functions in a lower one, called "anticipations." The latter assures that the functions "below" the analytical function (in the modal-functional order) have an intrinsic reference to the analytical function in anticipating this. The term "analogy" later came to be used to describe both retrocipations and anticipations of functions alike (2005d/e: §59).

In the second place, besides the subject-functions, a different kind of function is introduced, so-called "object-functions." These are functions of relevance in light of and in dependence upon subject-functions. E.g., humans and animals have sense-organs enabling them to perceive things, irrespective of whether the thing seen itself perceives. In being

---

60 Most of the following remarks appeal to Vollenhoven's *Isagôgè Philosophiae* (2005d/e; or the text-critical edition, including all the versions from 1930 on, Vollenhoven 2010.)

61 These individuals are usually thought of as being material things, plants, animals, and human beings. But in *Isagôgè Philosophiae* spatial forms and the natural numbers are also considered to be individuals. All these individuals, except numbers, can be perceived. The exception of numbers may be remedied (I believe) by taking a concrete set, that exemplifies a number, to be the perceptible component here. E.g., if one can perceive the size and shape of a book – its spatial form – why not consider the set of its pages as numerically perceptible?

perceived they fulfill the role of object of perception. Or: food sold on the market has an economic value for human beings, who determine this economic value in connection with scarcity or plenitude; the food is here an economic object, for it lacks an actual economic function of intrinsically fixed value. These two kinds of functions, object-functions and subject-functions, are predicated on individuals, but at the same time as "nestled in" in the vertical or ontological dimension of the law-spheres.

Thirdly, the logical law-sphere, which provided the logical schema of a relation with its terms, is now more focused on the analytical role. This function *distinguishes* what is different and *connects* what is common (or can be related). States of affairs, initially said to be the logical analogy (as relational network) in non-logical law-spheres, are now simply identical to whatever is the case at each modal level of the spheres. A relational network is thereby intrinsic to a law-sphere. That network is now no longer seen specifically as the "logical analogy" but as denoting intramodal features generally. The logical subject-function of distinguishing and connecting is performed in virtue of the terms and relations being structurally present (as states of affairs) in the law-sphere concerned. This logical subject-function notes and selects states of affairs, the latter being what is "analyzable," hence in the role of "logical object-function."[62] This forms the basis of concept formation and providing predicates of judgments (2005d/e: §175).

Then, perception is no longer taken to be "diametrically opposed" to knowing. Not everything is evident as to the reasons for this change, so a discussion of the problem cannot take place here. Suffice it to say that the change is evident in a refashioning of the horizontal dimension (determinant) generally. The horizontal determinant is fundamentally about connections between individuals. Vollenhoven erected a complex relational network in which concrete individual things and persons are taken to participate. Many kinds of relationships are distinguished, such as inter-individual, intra-individual, outer, inner, contemporary, successive, genetic, etc. The horizontal feature that is important to perception and knowing, as captured in the "act-content schema" of 1926, is now contextualized in the network of horizontal relationships. The theme of truth, so evident in the work of 1926, is no longer so overt. It would appear that the contextualization now includes the role of providing sat-

---

62   Here we are assuming our human habitat as the means of knowing. We cannot directly analyze what is beyond our "natural" range, such as divinity and the law as boundary of created reality, nor even the created heavens, short of being dependent on the means of revelation; cf. Vollenhoven 2005d/e: §173.

isfying conditions for the horizontal relation between knowing agent and knowable referent.

In conclusion, the shift of the position of the logical law-sphere did not diminish Vollenhoven's criticism of the traditional *logos*-doctrine. In fact, in his later historical work, particularly in the context of the problem-historical method, the categories of cosmic opposition and cosmic contrast have a central place in his use of the terms "dualism" and "monism" respectively. Vollenhoven remained unswerving in his appeal to an integral understanding of reality, in which fundamental bifurcations and oppositional splits are ruled out. Human life deserves better than to be subject to the false strictures that much traditional thought has put in the way.

As to *ratio*, the cognitive use of the "logical possibilities" that reality itself provides became more nuanced for Vollenhoven, all the while continuing to avoid rationalism and humanism. Throughout there is the appeal to the logical law-sphere. This means that there are norms (laws or principles) that control our thinking, not rigidly in prescribed forms, but by way of duty – the duty here being "to analyze whatever is analyzable, well" (1948p: 30). This is no invitation to rationalism, let alone humanism, for there are other duties too, meaning that there are other law-spheres of equal importance, though in each case as geared to its own kind of norms.

When, in compliance to the logical norm, one now peruses what there is to analyze, one finds in each law-sphere a wealth of states of affairs, potentially infinite and too rich to oversee. One honors divinity not in identifying this infinitude with the divine nature (as a possible understanding of theism might propose) – a nature that is in any case beyond our ken, in being unbounded – but in confessing and recognizing this infinitude to be inherent in God's creation work (§103). True, states of affairs don't "come to be and pass away." But behind genesis there is creation, of which states of affairs are a part.

Finally, there is the optimal use of logically discerned possibilities in the human striving to know. Discerned states of affairs – not necessarily merely the "logical" ones, pertaining to the make-up of relationships – are indispensable in meeting our epistemic interest. Concepts and judgments, of whatever modality, are formed through our handling of discerned states of affairs. Vollenhoven's approach to "Reformed epistemology" was to project the knowledge we come to, when forming concepts and judgments, against the background of cosmic (vertical and horizontal) dimensions or determinants. Truth shifted in his revised work from condition of epistemic satisfaction to the ontology of cosmic structure as such. After all, knowledge will itself not be structured aright – i.e., it will go rationally awry – when one gets that cosmic structure wrong (cf. Vollenhoven 2005d/e: §182).

Bibliography

Dooyeweerd, H. (1922), "Normatieve rechtsleer" (typescript). *Dooyeweerd Archives* 77, Box VN 38, Folder VIN 122. Amsterdam: Historisch Documentatiecentrum, Free University.

———— (1953), *A New Critique of Theoretical Thought*, vol. 1, trans. by D.H. Freeman and W.S. Young. Amsterdam: H.J. Paris; Philadelphia: Presbyterian and Reformed Publ. Co.

Girard, R. (1986), *The Scapegoat*, Baltimore: Johns Hopkins University Press.

James, W. (1992) [1907], "Pragmatism," in *Pragmatism in Focus*, ed. by D. Olin. London and New York: Routledge.

Klapwijk, J. (1980), "Honderd jaar filosofie aan de Vrije Universiteit," in *Wetenschap en Rekenschap 1880–1980. Een eeuw wetenschapsbeoefening en wetenschapsbeschouwing aan de Vrije Universiteit*, ed. by M. van Os and W.J. Wieringa. Kampen: Kok, 528–593.

Kok, J.H. (1992), *Vollenhoven: His early development*. Sioux Center, Iowa: Dordt College Press.

Kreiter, B.G. (Erik) (2007), *Philosophy as Weltanschauung in Trendelenburg, Dilthey and Windelband*. Dissertation Amsterdam: Vrije Universiteit.

Levinas, E. (1985), *Ethics and Infinity*, trans. by R.A. Cohen. Pittsburgh: Duquesne University Press.

Russell, B. (1919), *Introduction to Mathematical Philosophy*. London: Allen and Unwin.

Stellingwerff, J. (1992), *D.H.Th. Vollenhoven (1892–1978). Reformator der Wijsbegeerte*. Baarn: Ten Have.

Tol, A. (1995), "Time and change in Vollenhoven," *Philosophia Reformata* 60, 99–120.

———— (2010), *Philosophy in the Making: D.H.Th. Vollenhoven and the Emergence of Reformed Philosophy*. Sioux Center, Iowa: Dordt College Press.

———— (2011a), "Reformational Philosophy in the Making," *Philosophia Reformata* 76, 187–215.

———— (2011b), "Vollenhoven on Philosophy, Worldview and Religion," website: www.christelijkefilosofie.nl

Tol, A. and K.A. Bril (1992), *Vollenhoven als Wijsgeer. Inleidingen en Teksten*. Amsterdam: Buijten en Schipperheijn.

Van der Laan , H. (2000), *Jan Woltjer (1849–1917). Filosoof, Classicus, Pedagoog*. Amsterdam: VU Uitgeverij.

Van Riessen, H. (1959), *Op wijsgerige wegen*. Wageningen: Zomer & Keunings.

Vollenhoven, D.H.Th. (1918a), *De Wijsbegeerte der Wiskunde van Theïstisch*

Standpunt. Amsterdam: Van Soest.

———— (1921c), "Hegel op onze lagere scholen?" *Paedagogisch Tijdschrift voor het Christelijk Onderwijs* 14, 77–87, 99–106.

———— (1925c), "Een plant van eigen boden," *Paedagogisch Tijdschrift voor het Christelijk Onderwijs* 18, 391–394.

———— (1926a), *Logos and ratio: beider verhouding in de geschiedenis der Westersche kentheorie*. Kampen: Kok; 77 pgs.

———— (1926b), "Enkele grondlijnen der kentheorie," *Stemmen des Tijds* 15 (April), 380–401.

———— (1926d), "Kentheorie en natuurwetenschap," *Orgaan der Christelijke Vereeniging van Natuur- en Geneeskundigen in Nederland* (no. 2 and 4), 53–64, 147–197.

———— (1926msA), "Philosophia Systematica I (Kentheorie) 1926–1927" (Lecture notes), *Vollenhoven Archives* 405, Box 5. Amsterdam: Historisch Documentatiecentrum, Vrije Universiteit.

———— (1926msC), "De wijsbegeerte der arithmetiek en der chorologie van Calvinistisch standpunt," *Vollenhoven Archives* 405, Box 5. Amsterdam: Historisch Documentatiecentrum, Vrije Universiteit.

———— (1927msA), "Philosophia Systematica II (Kentheorie): 1927–1928" (Lecture notes), *Vollenhoven Archives* 405, Box 5. Amsterdam: Historisch Documentatiecentrum, Vrije Universiteit.

———— (1948p), *Hoofdlijnen der Logica*. Kampen: Kok.

———— (2005b), *The Problem-Historical Method and the History of Philosophy*, ed. by K.A. Bril, trans. by J. de Kievit, S. Francke, J.G. Friesen and R. Sweetman. Amstelveen: De Zaak Haes.

———— (2005d) [1945], *Isagôgè Philosophiae / Introduction to Philosophy*, ed. by John H. Kok and Anthony Tol, trans. by John H. Kok with a preface by Calvin Seerveld and a foreword by Anthony Tol. Sioux Center: Dordt College Press. (Bilingual Dutch-English edition)

———— (2005e), *Introduction to Philosophy*; separate English translation of Vollenhoven (2005d), with same preface and foreword.

———— (2010), *Isagôgè Philosophiae 1930–1945 tekstkritische uitgave. Filosofie in de Traditie van de Reformatie*, ed. by A. Tol. Amsterdam: Free University Press.

Whitehead, A.N. and B. Russell (1927) [1st ed. 1910], *Principia Mathematica*, volume 1. Cambridge: At the University Press.

Woldring, H.E.S. (2013), *Een handvol filosofen. Geschiedenis van de filosofiebeoefening aan de Vrije Universiteit in Amsterdam van 1880 tot 2012*. Hilversum: Verloren.

Woltjer, J. and A. Kuyper (1895), *Publicatie van den Senaat der Vrije Universiteit, in zake het onderzoek ter bepaling van den weg die tot de kennis der Gereformeerde beginselen leidt*, J. Woltjer, rector, A. Kuyper, abactis. Amsterdam: Wormser.

Logos and *Ratio*

> For the great obstacle hindering the development of epistemology was and continues to be the lack of analysis.
>
> D.H.Th. Vollenhoven (§166)

"Most welcome listeners"♦

A. *Introduction*

(§1) When I call your attention this afternoon to the discussion of the relation of *logos* and *ratio* as prevalent in Western thought of different centuries, you will realize that my topic belongs to the area of *epistemology*. But then I also fear that your first impression is likely to be to consider the topic ill-chosen, for it lies so remote from daily life. Some might venture to ask: "Wasn't there, in the broad area of the disciplines entrusted to you, something else to find deserving urgent attention? Doesn't psychology in particular wrestle with countless unsolved issues, and wouldn't addressing one of these difficulties have offered a better opportunity to come to a well-rounded conclusion?"

(§2) Such questions have legitimacy, as I immediately acknowledge, at least in part. Yet, in my opinion, epistemology deserved precedence. This is for the following reasons.

(§3) First of all, from an encyclopedic perspective, this special discipline of epistemology deserves preference to a discussion of a topic that might also be less encompassing, precisely because its questions – often unnoticed by the specialist – recur in every field of inquiry. Other difficulties, however urgently they demand a solution, can thus only benefit when these fundamental problems are addressed first.

(§4) Then there is an entirely different motive that contributes its share

---

♦ [Immediately prior to this general greeting Vollenhoven addressed those present according to the different bodies represented, namely, Directors of the Association that sponsors the university, Curators of the university, Chaired professors, Doctors of a discipline, Ministers of the Word, Students: ladies and gentlemen, and "also all of you who came to honor this ceremony with your presence." At the end of his presentation (from §208 on) he specifically addresses these groups (except the last mentioned).]

in choosing to address precisely this topic. For it cannot be denied that, apart from systematic interest, also in our time – and in particular in our Reformed life – addressing epistemological difficulties is a pressing demand. For current philosophy is either [/6] life-philosophy, which becomes averse to any reflection on scientific difficulties, or it courses in a logistically one-sided way that exaggerates the meaning of science and forbids every journey outside of the Hercules columns of the formalistic channel. The antipathy against the second standpoint often increases the attractiveness of the first, also for those who, in light of their Reformed point of departure, could know better.

These circumstances sometimes lead the most cautious provisionally to circumvent the greatest difficulties. One is "provisionally" satisfied with pursuing more specialist work, which not only leads to quicker practical results, but in addition offers the advantage of being lenient to a certain piety that marks clarity of concepts as rationalistic. There needs to be an urgent warning against this avoidance, also from the side of our university: not only from out of an enlightened self-interest, but also no less for the sake of the whole of Reformed life. For unless this defeatism is not forcefully called to a timely halt, the Reformed awakening will soon be exchanged for a hibernation deeper than any seen up to now.

(§5) The combination of these two motives induced me to shift the focus of my interest, which was constantly aimed especially at epistemological questions, only just a little, namely from systematic reflection to historical considerations. I did this neither exclusively for you, who would probably welcome for the most part an historical introduction above that of a systematic exposition, nor from a personal desire to exchange, for once, more demanding work for an overview that is less taxing to the mental powers. For the goal is certainly not merely to relate historical details recently discovered; rather, the beckoning ideal for me continued to be that of deepening my own systematic insight, also in connection with historical research; and doing so in two ways: by being prompted to be doubly careful when coming across questionable consequences, and by being less prone to succumb to one-sidedness (always a threat) through contact with neglected [historical] moments. In that way, the method automatically became a pragmatic one, and the critique remained transcendent, even though it appeared that operating with our own distinctions often made it possible to gain a sharper insight into the immanent development of many a system as well.

(§6) I hope that, backed by these introductory remarks, the choice of my topic will be justified, namely, *Logos and ratio: their relation in the history of Western epistemology.*

B. *Ancient philosophy*

(§7) *Logos* and *ratio*♦ – they need to be clearly distinguished and yet are closely related. Their distinction is intimately tied in, as are all boundary problems, with the answers to the following questions: "What serves as the *principium divisionis* [principle of division] of the chief partition [of reality]?" and "Where ought, in consequence, the chief incision to be applied that controls all the remaining distinctions?"

(§8) For example – returning for a moment to that period of Greek history when there was as yet no epistemology in a specific sense to speak of [/7] – whoever accepts, as in Homer's sphere of influence, the rule of fate has no choice but to draw the chief boundary between this unfathomable and that which is controlled by it, including both gods and human beings. This kind of epic dualism is of course naturalistic in its theory [*leer*]■ concerning God, and its view of the human being is both fatalistic and optimistic, namely, humanity needs to bow submissively to fate, but then again it shares this [state] equally with the gods.

(§9) Whoever on the contrary rejects fate – or never accepted it – favors a monism [i.e., a holism] that is either definitive or makes room for pure dualism, namely a dualism between God, who instates His ordinances, and the cosmos, which stands under these laws.

(§10) In this connection it should be noted that monism is compatible with many forms of impure dualism, all of which pretend to be able to replace the correct chief partition, but in so doing lack a sufficient basis. Consequently, either one exaggerates the meaning of a sub-division and takes a reference of provincial distinction to be the federal boundary, or one raises a fence that totally ignores the nature of what it encloses. The latter is of course totally wrong, [while] the first error often hinders making fruitful use of what as such is perhaps in itself an important discovery. In the development of Western epistemology one comes across many examples of both mistakes.

♦[Neither "*logos*" nor "*ratio*" is made explicit in this and the following three paragraphs; one might consult §49, §55, and §66; A.T.]

■[The term "leer" can also mean "doctrine" or "teaching." Thus, unless stated otherwise, the use of "theory" in this translation should be taken in a broad rather than a restrictive, merely scientific sense; A.T.]

1. *Pre-Socratics*

(§11) As far as we know the development of Western epistemology began with the enormous change that mysticism apparently set in motion in many parts of the world in the seventh century B.C. In the East this change led to ceding the victory to the infinite; [but] the Greeks, being of a different disposition, looked for boundary and measure.[1]

(§12) Now this [change in mysticism] did mean that the dualistic view of Homer – at least to the extent that it had been influential – had to yield to monism. But this did not exclude the distinction between the human being and its environment: pantheistic mysticism, which rejects the distinction between God and cosmos, leads in the long run to the humanistic dualism of subject and object. Hence this dualism does not combat religious monism, but differs from it only in making a typically Western appraisal of the human being more explicit; for which there is certainly a place within pure dualism, but which became dangerous in overlooking the principal boundary.

(§13) With the Ionian "nature philosophers"[2] the emphasis still falls very strongly on the unity of the human being with the world. One finds the same emphasis in Heraclitus too, the Nietzsche of antiquity. Heraclitus identifies the principle sought by his predecessors – some of whom had already noted the differentiation [of a dominant cosmic element, such as water, air, etc.] according to distinct processes – as the conflict of opposites. In this way a triadic system of unity arises.

Less well-known is that the first philosophy of the *logos* [namely that of Heraclitus] offers little more than preaching about the individual human being's undergoing this trinitarian process. [/8] Even Diels, in his *Vorsokratiker* [*Pre-Socratics*], still failed to observe the difference between *logos* [effective word, authoritative speech] and *epos* [story, saga]; and yet precisely here lies the kernel of Heraclitus' philosophy of language.[3] For

---

1   K. Joël, *Geschichte der antiken Philosophie*, I (Tübingen: Mohr [Paul Siebeck], 1921), 149–227. [This development is usually referred to as the Axial Age; cf. Karin Armstrong, *The Great Transformation* (London: Atlantic Books, 2006); A.T.]

2   On the incorrectness of this characterization, currently generally acknowledged, see what Dr. R.H. Woltjer already noted in his *Het mystiek religieuse element in de Griek-sche philologie*. Inaugural address, Faculty of Arts and Philosophy, Free University, Friday 23 September 1904 (Leiden: Donner, 1905); passim, especially 13 and 25.

3   H. Diels, *Die Fragmente der Vorsokratiker, Griechisch und Deutsch*, 3rd ed., I (Berlin:

[N.B. The footnotes are transferred from endnotes, beginning on page 71 of the original printed text; A.T.]

according to him the *logos* is the articulated sentence, the reason, the argument, which takes up into itself the distinct words, moments, and objections, thereby transforming them into concepts; and in this synthesis [the *logos*] offers the powerful expression of the world process that the soul undergoes.[4] The Dorians subordinate the spoken word to number, but the thought of "undergoing" is certainly also not lost on them.

2. *Socrates*

(§14) This view, as though the *logos* became immanently conscious for the human being, is connected quite early in the West with the thought that the human being controls his environment through calculation and even more through speech. In the Pre-Socratics this combination is linked to the identification of thought and spoken judgment, the latter being taken as sentence. Forming a judgment is thought to be purely mystical; forming the content of the judgment, i.e., of knowledge, is not yet a problem for any of these philosophers.

They also overlooked the spheres in which a cosmic unity, such as a human being, only appears to the extent that it is subject to the laws of these spheres. For "subject" will soon mean, also for the disputatious Sophists, "(placed or) thrown under," though not [under] the law, but rather as subjected to the weight of the objection raised by the opponent, which must then be decisively waylaid. In this way "subject" acquires the meaning of "bearer of activity," and "object" that of "resistance as endured by this bearer" – [the latter] of course as expressed in another *judgment*.[5]

Socrates shares these assumptions but deepens the view of a judgment appreciably by distinguishing the boldness with which it is asserted and the ground on which it rests. As long as one may not ask about the latter, judgment is opinion, a "non-knowing that" [*niet-weten*], and can only be called *true* when correlated with the concept. Thus the concept determines the value of the judgment.[6] Philosophy of language and logic are no longer on a par; a parting of ways that can only be beneficial to both.

(§15) So Socrates opposed the Sophists by insisting that the validity of a

---

Weidemann, 1912), 12, Band 1, 77.

4   Ernst Hoffmann, *Die Sprache und die archaische Logik* (Tübingen: Mohr [Paul Siebeck], 1925), 1–8.

5   E. Alberti, "Die Sprachphilosophie vor Platon," *Philologus* 11 (Göttingen: Dieterich, 1856): 681–705.

6   Richard Hönigswald, *Die Philosophie des Altertums. Problem-geschichtliche und systematische Untersuchungen* (München: Reinhardt, 1917), 123 ff.

judgment be secured. He was so convinced of the moral character of his mission that he held that one may only speak of concept formation in the context of morality. In doing so he confused the relationship of concept to judgment with the relationship between that about which a concept is formed and the formed concept. Now, although this [confusion] undoubtedly is to be censured, it should be noted that a concept does indeed pose a demand on some judgments. In view of the course of history it is, true enough, easy to understand that Socrates proceeded from the judgment and ended with the concept. However, for epistemology this course of affairs has been disastrous. For, although the correlation of concept and judgment is undeniable in many cases, one ought not to forget that it is not universal, as is evident in connection with judgments of existence or discerning. In addition, [/9] the concept◆ is a result of grasping; one grasps something with something, a content with the aid of a form. But precisely this orientation to a judgment makes it easy to forget what the concept is in its essence, namely *truth* grasped in a *form*. Two confusions go hand in hand here: (i) that of the truth of a judgment and truth as such, and (ii) that of non-conceptual and conceptual knowledge, i.e., of unformed and formed truth possession. Socrates is more concerned with judgment formation on the basis of knowledge already formed than with the essence of the latter – which is why he can correctly apply the figure of a midwife.

(§16) All these errors hang together with the monistic point of departure, linked to the overrating of the human being. There is first of all the opinion that the region for concept formation is of a moral nature, i.e., there is but one terrain, namely that on which the human being plays an active role, including that of pronouncing judgment [*oordeelvellend*]. In virtue of this monism the judgment of discerning is irrelevant: neither this judgment nor the intuition correlated to it has value when one does not accept different terrains. As a result, the concept, now bereft of its natural trail blazer, in fact comes to stand entirely on its own. Then, apparently sensing this to be unsatisfactory, the concept is linked to perception, adduced by every philosopher who proceeds from "what there is to see" as surrogate for discerning. The point of departure for concept formation is then not the discerned modality of the circle of consideration [*gezich-*

◆ [*Begrip* is a result of *grijpen*. As John Kok pointed out to me, this use of *concept*, where a concept is the result of *grasping*, may be compared with *concept* from Medieval Latin *conceptum* "draft, abstract," which is from, in classical Latin, *concept-*, past participle stem of *concipere* "to take in."]

tsveld], but the *object* (of perception). From the time of Socrates, epistemology has never broken the spell of this subject-object schema, and the attempt of a solitary individual[7] to escape from its control was doomed, by virtue of the point of departure of humanism, to fail from the start.

(§17) But there is still more to say as result of being laced in this straitjacket [of the subject-object schema]. For concept and representation [of perception] differ *toto caelo* [diametrically]. Now, one who holds that a concept is the result of grasping-truth-in a-distinct-form, and maintains that both the truth and the form in question are independent of the subject, is able to account for this difference. When perceiving, the human subject creates individually different, more or less free reproductions of a perceived figure. On the other hand, although bringing a form and content together, i.e., conceiving, calls for activity on the part of the individual, the connection of form and content is not characterized by individuality. But whoever is of the opinion that the concept finds its origin in perceptions and representations has no option but to attempt to account for this difference [between perceiving and conceiving] in a totally skewed way. A concept's being supra-personal and representations personal are taken as standing to each other in the [human] subject as general and particular. Because this difference needs to be secured somehow, one looks for a basis in the object, where the same difference is induced, namely, that which is general – this being in correlation [/10] with the concept in the subject – controls a larger area than what is particular, of which perception is supposed to give an account.

3. *Plato*
(§18) Plato built on the foundation as laid. Although he does not limit concept formation to the ethical terrain, his early dialogues are still primarily about judgment truth. However, he also subjects the anthropological concept of the subject to further analysis, concluding that not everything here is homogeneous; after all, in sense-perception the human being is passive – the original activity is evident only in knowledge by concepts. Yet the schema of subject–environment, if it is to remain harmonious, calls for [acknowledging] something twofold in the perceived object that is parallel to the duality in the subject. To that end the object is first approached anthropomorphically, such that it contains, in a way similar to a human being, an inner and an outer [side]. The outer is the appearing that appeals to the senses; the inner is the essence that is

---

7   Cf. e.g., the attempt ventured by R. Herbertz, in his *Prolegomena zu einer realistischen Logik* (Halle: Niemeyer, 1916).

known through concepts. So, what Socrates called "general" is for Plato "essential," over against which the "particular" is then reduced to the rank of "appearing." In that way concepts are honored as being the key enabling us to penetrate into the secrets hidden behind the appearing.

(§19) In these statements truth and error are very closely knit. The predicate "not perceivable by the senses" can indeed be attributed to truths as well, hence also to knowledge, whether conceptual [i.e., formed] or not conceptual [i.e., unformed]. But while this predicate, in being negative, is all-inclusive – excluding only what is perceptible by the senses – it is not at all suited for a positive reference. For there is much more than truth and knowledge that is not perceptible by the senses, also among that about which a truth is a truth.

(§20) The error resides in the anthropological approach [*anthropologiseering*]. In the human being the functions of perception and knowing do indeed go hand in hand, and correlate to these are perceived objects and truths. But the latter two don't relate to each other as appearing and essence. An essence is a cosmic unity [e.g., an individual], and some truths, namely metaphysical ones, are indeed truths about essences. But there are many truths that are not about essences [per se], but about intersections of essences, namely about essences insofar as they lie in a distinct law-sphere. In connection with knowledge one distinguishes knowledge by intuition and knowledge by concepts. Parallel to this is the division of judgments in existence judgments and relation judgments. But the judgment of existence or of discerning should not be identified with the judgment of perception, for to perceive is not [the same as] to know, and an essence is not correlate with a concept. In the most favorable case – namely in metaphysics – it is correlate with a moment of a concept, while this moment can, by continued investigation, become a system.

(§21) The consequences were dire, even for psychology. Perception was indeed not yet robbed, as in Aristotle, of its own [/11] value. But what we do have is that the understanding of one function among many [namely, the cognitive function] – one that cannot operate at all without aids – was raised to be the magic wand that forced the "inner side of nature" to reveal its treasures.

(§22) Knowledge is then the content of a judgment, which is described as a community of concepts, that is actualized by synthetic thought. But knowing is truth-possession: it is *systasis*, not synthesis, indeed [a] condition but certainly not [an] act. The synthesis referenced here occurs neither in knowing nor in the process of coming-to-know, but only in concept formation, which is the connecting of truth-moments in a form. Whoever transfers to knowing the connecting that goes into forming concepts will end up equating formed truth [concepts] and truth-possessed [knowledge]. That is why Plato's *erôs* [desire] remains caught in the same strictures as the later mysticism in his wake: one seeks the security of truth in the certainty of its possession. So too Augustine in confusing [the cognitive] "knowing that" ["*weten dat*"] and the psychical "know of" ["*weet van*"] can legitimately appeal to Plato, who speaks in the *Charmides* of "having knowledge of one's (cognitive) knowing (that)" ["*weet hebben van het (kennend) weten (dat)*"].[8] [We add that] Augustine's "knowing that" is to us the same as "knowing of" ["*kennen van*"], with the emphasis on the certainty of possession rather than on the security of truth.

(§23) But Plato's confusion between truth and truth-possession considerably warps the theory of knowledge in yet another way. For something is represented in truth and thus also in knowledge – i.e., in the whole of knowledge, hence in both the idea and the concept – that is not as such of a logical nature; e.g., that which is psychical in psychological [truth or knowledge]. However, this holds equally for both general and particular concepts. Hence the metaphysical founding of truth can never be a subpart of classifying the particular under the general. Besides, "general" and "particular" can only be discovered through comparison. In contrast, truth's representative character, which is not established by means of comparison, holds independently of the result to which research, or the specific moments of truth recurring in two or more concepts [when compared], leads. To state it differently: the analogy of the logical is present in every law-sphere, but each time transformed; and this "being present everywhere," which rests on the cosmic order of the distinct [law-] spheres, is not of the same order as, say, the generality of the point's recurring in every mathematical figure.

(§24) The anthropocentric point of departure however also dominates the view of *logos* and *mathesis*. According to the *Theaetetus* both should be ranked with knowing. Now certainly no knowing is possible without the logical [factor], but *mathesis* itself requires that the logical is nevertheless not placed on a par with mathematics. By virtue of the cosmic order –

---

8   Plato, *Charmides* 164D, 165C, 166C – E. von Aster, *Platon* (Stuttgart: Strecker und Schröder, 1925), 77 ff. In connection with the rejection on the basis of the apparent – Plato would say "evident" – *regressus ad indefinitum* [regression to the indefinite], cf. R. Herbertz, *Das philosophische Urerlebnis* (Bern und Leipzig: Bircher, 1921), 41 ff.

in which the mathematical [sphere] precedes the physical [sphere] – an analogy of the mathematical does occur in the succeeding spheres. But even though number is invisible, that does not give one the right to draw it into the [/12] mind [*geest*]. Especially later, when the subject-object schema supplants metaphysics, it will be evident to what disconcerting consequences this leads.

(§25) On the credit side of the *Theaetetus* one may note that this dialogue distinguishes reflection and the decision based on it – i.e., pronouncing a judgment and what precedes it – from knowledge. The bond between discourse, which remains closely associated with judgment, and knowledge has become less firm; [in short] dialectic cannot have the final say.[9]

4. *Aristotle*

(§26) The preceding indicates the development prior to the Aristotelian distinction between dialectic and theory of proof, the first of which belongs to the theory of judgment. Now how does the "father of logic" come to his view of the *apodeigma* [demonstration]? He proceeds from the dualism of his teacher between idea and sensory appearing, which he tries to reduce to a unity. However, the manner in which he proceeds clearly reveals his anthropocentric approach. Though himself a biologist, he does not ask which method is appropriate to his field of inquiry, but describes, in typical Greek fashion, what is visibly seen, [namely] the spatial form of the mature specimen of a species. For the thing is a form that realizes itself; [it is] an organism that completely realizes itself in its material appearance only when it is mature, in the same way that it is itself the realization of a higher organic unity, the species. The base of this *form-matter* pyramid is unformed matter, the breeding ground of the "accidental"; the top is the immaterial form, the Aristotelian idol, namely hypostasized self-consciousness.[10] As in Plato, the thinker of Stagira shares the humanistic neglect of the difference in emphasis between "knowing" ["*kennen*"] and "knowing that" ["*weten, dat*"] and likewise [the neglect] of the distinction between "knowing that" ["*weten, dat*"] and "know(ing)/have knowledge of" ["*weet van*"], in which more is relevant than just a difference in emphasis [in being cognitive and psychical respectively]. However, Aristotle's accepting self-consciousness in a non-psychical sense, something his teacher rejected, follows from the difference in point of departure: the duality in Plato becomes a bi-unity in the

---

9   Hoffmann, *Die Sprache und die archaische Logik*, 77.

10   W. Windelband (A. Bonhöffer), *Geschichte der antiken Philosophie*, 3rd ed. (München: Beck, 1912), 231.

disciple.[11]

(§27) Between these two extremes of formless matter and immaterial form there is *inter alia* the human being, in connection with whom the form-matter schema is also consistently applied. Of greatest interest for our topic is the distinction of active and passive *nous* [intellect]. Under the *nous* is the soul with its duality of *anima vegetativa* [nutritive soul] and *anima sensitiva* [sensitive soul]. To the latter he ascribes perception, as based on desire and motion. The synthesis of the sense-data of the different sense organs lies in the central [i.e., common] sense. The *nous* is not a part of the soul but it is its form, itself superseded only, as matter, by the divine form of self-consciousness. In the human individual, however, this *nous* is only in a stage of development, which is why one can also further distinguish here in form and matter, namely between the *nous poieticos* [active or creating mind] and the *nous patheticos* [feeling or undergoing/experiencing mind]. The latter is the animal soul *as* matter for the former.[12] [/13]

(§28) The epistemology that Aristotle now develops further is completely in line with this biological metaphysics. The object of knowing is no longer the ontic♦ idea but the biotic unity of species, which appears in the specimen. General representations arise in the soul through the tarrying of impressions out of what nowadays is called "the biotic absolute medium" (Driesch).[13] General representations are, in turn, the material for concepts.

(§29) Perception, unlike in Plato, is degraded to be the transition point of knowing. For the species realizes itself in the specimen, which is what is perceived, such that perceptions in the [knowing] subject are to the concept what the material is to its form. Thus the form-matter schema has the final say both within and outside of the subject. And over against that subject, with its different levels, stands the object, with an essentially similar layered structure.

---

11   Herbertz, *Das philosophische Urerlebnis*, 41–50.

12   Windelband, *Geschichte der antiken Philosophie*, 235–240.

13   H. Driesch, *Der Begriff der organischen Form, Abhandlungen zur theoretischen Biologie*, herausgegeben von Julius Schaxel in Jena, Heft 3 (Berlin: Gebrüder Bornträger, 1919), 15–35.

♦[Reading "ontische" for "ontolische" (*sic*). The Platonic idea is itself a being that, as an essence separate from sensory things, controls their appearances; A.T.]

(§30) Thus a concept is here, by virtue of its origin, a form that typifies appearances, hence [a form] of phenotypical "characteristics." Now one should not underestimate the value of arranging phenomena for practical life in this way; e.g., consider the identifying marks used in descriptions, etc. But may one in such cases then speak of a *concept*? In illustrating this question I intentionally choose an example of biological classification. Suppose: I have a plant catalogued in my "Herbarium." Then I know that I'm dealing with a plant that belongs to the class of objects as sketched in this typology. Do I now also know that it belongs to the same species as a second plant of the same class? Aristotle thought this was the case. But more recent biology has brought to light that phenotype similarity gives absolutely no right to assert genotype kinship. In other words, in the very field of inquiry for which this theory was initially designed, it appeared to be untenable. Thus concept formation is not to be replaced by the description of a spatial form, nor is asserting genealogical connection [replaceable] by registering the points of agreement between graphically stilled forms.

(§31) But our critique of this theory of concept formation [in Aristotle] needs to penetrate yet more deeply.

(§32) First of all, as regards the *object*. Biotic reality is not a thing-essence and physical reality is not appearance. Biology and physics are as sciences completely on a par, although the biotic field [of inquiry] rests, in view of the biological method, on [that] of physics. And these fields are intersections of the cosmos, such that a cosmic unity – which is what an essence actually is – is present in different fields.

(§33) And as to the *subject*, one needs to distinguish sharply representation and concept. Representing is an act, and acts can succeed each other; representations are images that are brought about in these acts. In this work of reproducing the soul can follow the model fairly slavishly or only [/14] loosely; and later on the results can again be magnified, connected, isolated, etc. But all the while they remain a faithful or not so faithful copy of an object of perception. With a concept, in contrast, there is also an act, but not one aimed at what is perceived. For the activity of the soul consists here of grasping a truth-content in a truth-form, neither of which *arises* owing to perception. Rather the processing [of what is conceived] begins by discerning both [truth features], but this discerning of intuition is not in the least equivalent to perception.

(§34) Then finally there is the *relationship* of subject and object. Both are [in Aristotle] subject to the pan-vitalistic teleological whole, whose schema recurs in the one as well as in the other. The concept here never pertains to more than one object, which, being the *species*, includes already in itself the determination of the scope of its region.

(§35) But of course the theory of the *apodeigma* [demonstration] involves more than [just] concept formation, for it rests on the combination of judgments. Now Aristotle too views judgment again exclusively in correlation with the concept. For according to him the terrain of concepts is completely congruent with the scope of knowledge. Thus his faulty theory of the concept also has an adverse effect on his theory of judgment. Failing to distinguish form and content in the concept, he cannot subsume negation under what is merely the undertaken (and thus not yet completed) combining of this form with its content. Likewise he fails to recognize "the false" in the incorrectly executed combination of these two. So both negation and falsehood are associated with judgment.[14]

(§36) According to Aristotle a judgment is moreover in its essence always a connection of two concepts, connected in such a way that it subsumes the lower [concept], as subject or material, under a higher [concept], as predicate or form. Judgment is always subsumption judgment, and the simplest schema is: S is P.

Although this logic of the judgment may be widely accepted, it is not on that account correct. Its entire foundation crumbles with the metaphysics on which it rests. For first of all, judgments of existence don't subsume, and precisely these judgments offer the simplest type of judgment. The schema "S is P" displays a much more composite structure, namely, a synthesis, not of concepts but of existence judgments, more specifically of the following two: "S is" and "P is." Separately each forms a complete judgment, and only when connected together do they yield a judgment of the Aristotelian type.[15] Existence is not a relation; hence an existence judgment is not a relation judgment, and it ought not to be viewed as correlated to a concept. Besides, not every relation is class relation, hence this logic, though it has gained the stature of a classic, pertains to at most a small group of judgments, namely those that concern the scope of the regions of the combinations of characteristics.

---

14 Schalwa Nuzubidse, *Wahrheit und Erkenntnisstruktur, eine Einleitung in den aletheio-logischen Realismus* (Berlin und Leipzig: De Gruyter & Co., 1926), 117–120.

15 This view is in partial agreement with that of Brentano, who however associates representation and concept too closely. For a summary indication of his theory of judgment see F. Brentano, *Vom Ursprung sittlicher Erkenntnis* (Leipzig: Duncker & Humboldt, 1889), 51–52; cf. also note 141 below.

(§37) Hence Aristotle did not recognize judgment synthesis to be there where it is indeed to be found. Besides in language, he discovered it only in [/15] the syllogism. In virtue of the subsumptive nature of the premises of a syllogism, the latter leads to a conclusion that is again of the same form and of the same so-called metaphysical force [as the premises].

(§38) I reviewed this particular logic as extensively as I did because it is still accepted in many quarters. Its proponents often don't recognize [its disputable features:] the anthropocentric metaphysics; the pyramid structure of the form-matter schema, capped by its deified self-consciousness; the confusion of concept and general representation; and, on the basis of the latter, the confusion of a group of described graphic forms – organized according to the degree of vagueness of the described forms – with truth's coherence.

(§39) Hence this logic is anything but formal. Its main fault is not the surprising incompleteness – *nota bene*: knowing/conceiving is no more than a specific case of the ubiquitous form-content schema♦ – but rather the purely humanistic style in which this epistemology, and hence also the arm of logic, is constructed. No wonder, for here metaphysics speaks the language of a special science [i.e., biology], which in addition derives the boundary of its terrain from the historical opposition of [the states of being] dead or alive instead of from the appropriate distinctiveness [*eigensoortigheid*] of the divine law.

5. *Post-Aristotelian developments*
(§40) In the meantime, it was precisely "life" that became a threat to this system. For an individual does indeed stem from two other [individuals], but this birth is something totally different from the derivation of the smaller region of a class of $n+1$ characteristics out of a greater region of a group with n characteristics. In other words, the *concept* of the individual was soon privileged above that of the general concepts of species.

Two "corrections" of Theophrastus are telling here. In the first place, the particular judgment, which in Aristotle first occurs in the theory of the syllogism, is given a status that is entirely independent of the syllogism and is called "indeterminate."[16] Secondly, although the teacher [Aristotle] had equated them (correctly so from his standpoint), Theophrastus attempts to distinguish between *kath auto* [as such] and *he auto*

16   C. Prantl, *Geschichte der Logik im Abendlande*, I (Leipzig: S. Hirzel, 1855), 356.

♦[Presumably this ought to read "form-matter schema"; A.T.]

[in itself], such that the boundary between these two again lies in the individual thing.[17]

As a result, the term "abstract" gradually gains in meaning; first applied only to the side of the subject, it now also holds for the object, such that "general" becomes synonymous with "abstract." By virtue of the pyramid construction of the whole, what is now "abstract" in subject and object is soon equated, and as such comes to stand over against what is individual. Not only is that questionable for all matters social, it is no less so for epistemology. For neither truth nor concept is abstract. They only become so in a metaphysical sense when one is of the opinion that one can subjectively deduce these from perception and from the represented images formed in perception, and/or that they are objectively congruent with groups of described forms. The latter can indeed be abstract when they mark as equal what [in fact] is not at all equal for the concrete concept and the concrete truth. [/16]

(§41) The preference found among the older Peripatetics for the concept about that which is individual anticipated a link with so-called formal logic. Its birth had only to await the revitalization of the representation of the subject that had already characterized the fifth century BC. For, after all, wasn't it the same schema as applied in the object that is consequentially applied in the [knowing] subject?

6. *The Stoics*

(§42) Now, the Stoics preached the ethics of the individual who, regardless of his surroundings, simply lived in compliance with the world law. The application of this view to epistemology prevented them from appreciating the sound features that we found in their predecessors. Knowledge no longer remains distinct from judging; *dialectics* reclaims its status of old. Yes, even the gain, namely that the unformulated judgment is still something other than that to which language gives voice, escaped them, though they continue to distinguish making a judgment from the exchange of question and answer that precedes it. Dialectics is placed alongside rhetoric, and together they form the science of correct speech. The difference is purely psychological: the rhetorician speaks fluently, the dialectician succinctly.[18] Actually, the science of the latter lies in the lingual-philosophical domain; thus it can be classified purely linguistically into phonetics [the theory of sounds] and [semantics/significs, i.e.]

---

17   Prantl, *Geschichte der Logik im Abendlande*, 392.

18   Cicero, *De finibus* [i.e., *On Supreme Good and Evil*] II, 6, 17, cited in Prantl, *Geschichte der Logik im Abendlande*, 413.

the theory of *semainomena/significa* [or contextual meanings]. The latter meanings are identical to concepts.

In order not to underrate the potential of this Stoic theory of concepts, one should distinguish "to signify" ["*betekenen*"] and "to represent" ["*vertegenwoordigen*"]. "To signify" always presupposes a sign, though the state of affairs signified does not have to be perceptible by the senses, for a "sign" is not the same as a "design"/"drawing" ["*teekening*"]. But the sign itself is indeed inherently perceptible by the senses. However, in connection with concepts – as grasped *truth* – this is precisely excluded. For truth is always "truth about something," which [something] is accordingly represented in that truth. Name and concept may never be identified. But of course, one who fails to recognize the truth character of concepts and only has an eye for the moment of reference, such must find the agreement precisely in this respect between name and concept to be striking. But even then it need not be necessary to reduce a concept to a name; e.g., in Heraclitus the *logos* ennobles names to become *logos*-moments or concepts. But of course he reckons himself to be a prophet, and not he, but the world process brings this change in designation about in him. Not so the Stoic; he is the rhetorician. For him the *logos* is not a hyper-cosmic process, but a proof, and also this word means – very different than in Aristotle – a mere ranking of arguments. Each argument is a judgment, a spoken sentence, a *lexis*. Now an orator can exchange in such a judgment one or more words with a synonym, and thus this sentence is no more than a synthesis of words, of *lecta*. They only denote things but miss the character of truth. To what figure does truth apply? It applies to judgment, which is here neither a process nor a concept, but only offers the *synthesis* of concepts bereft of truth. And [yet] it is this synthesis that brings about truth [/17], without any change in the character of the elements.

(§43) The kernel of nominalism is not that it supposedly denies the reality of concepts. It does not even have to do this with respect to general concepts, nor with respect to their correlates in the object, the general species. It is only the substantiality – which the Stoics take to be the same as being bodily – of the former [i.e., general concepts] that is denied. No, the concept becomes a *name*; indeed a name as to which all truth character is denied. Irrespective of whatever moment of reference is present, the concept no longer offers *truth* about something.

(§44) So while there is regression to be noted as compared to Heraclitus, the decline is much greater when taking into account what Plato and

Aristotle taught. The recognition of this truth character occasioned their distinguishing the concept and the spoken word. But not only that. This insight was basic to the Platonic division of knowledge and perception; and although Aristotle leveled the characteristic difference between these two to a case of the ubiquitous form-content scheme,♦ the same insight restrained him from seriously considering the fatal abstraction theory [cf. §40]. Now while Theophrastus cannot be blamed for more than having expanded somewhat the [operational] terrain of the term "abstract," the doubtful credit of overturning the entire framework that separated concept and representation goes to the Stoics.

(§45) The consequences soon became evident. As for the *concept*, it seemed that the time was finally ripe to do justice to the process of concept formation. But with the connection of concept and truth broken, what remained was only a genetic account of – yes, of what? The notion of abstraction now reigned supreme, very soon attended upon by a kind of association biology. What passed for concepts, and could not be completely derived from representation, were taken to be evidently inborn in the individual. In the areas of religion, ethics, and aesthetics particularly one sought refuge in prolepsis [i.e., in the anticipatory relevance of these areas inherent in the mind].

(§46) And as for *truth*, truth was created in the synthesis of moments lacking truth, namely from inborn concepts and concepts abstracted from representations. This synthesis was executed by the individual human being, who could thus only use something immanent to himself as criterion, such as, e.g., the *firmness* of conviction.[19] Knowledge of the "external" world was secured through the evidence provided by immediately undergone sense-perception, which is only possible when the sense organs function properly and in the absence of real or internal obstacles.[20]

(§47) But when the human being climbed so high, thinking that he could perform divine work, a mysterious vertigo soon overcame him. And then it is wise to take stock. It is no wonder that, after this self-divination of the philosopher, skepticism, which preaches the sense of withholding judgment, spoke the word that was straight from the heart of the dead-tired person. [/18]

---

19   Prantl, *Geschichte der Logik im Abendlande,* 418.

20   Windelband, *Geschichte der antiken Philosophie,* 278 ff. [/72]

♦[Presumably this ought to read "form-matter schema"; A.T.]

C. *The Patristic period*

(§48) To this injured world, though it was far from healed of its haughtiness, Christianity was now brought, preaching grace above all else, but doing so on the basis of the revelation of God, which was in no way identified with that grace. For grace is forgiveness of sins, and sin is the theoretical or practical transgression of the law. Thus Christianity drew the line not between fate and that which is subject to it [cf. §8], nor between death and life [cf. §39], but between God and cosmos, between Law-giver and creature, which stands under the law [cf. §9].

(§49) If only it had been able to continue in this line. But life's pressing needs led to hasty action. Origen realized that religion spans all of life and thus also transcends science, but he did not design a new theory of knowledge. In this way Greek humanistic wisdom was simply incorporated, adjusted somewhat, and used immediately. After denying Stoicism's corporality of the *logos*, most entertained the sweet delusion that with that the *logos* concept of Holy Scripture was rightly understood! As if the Logos in Scripture wasn't exclusively divine, and that one didn't need to distinguish sharply between this Logos, of whom it once was said that He "was coming into the world" and for the sake of which He gave His life, and [on the other hand] "the logical [law-sphere]," which, when viewed intuitively, grants us the schema that – as *organon* – brings formed truth into our possession. When calling Himself the Truth, this entails either that He relates to the promise as that which is promised[21] or [that He is] the full revelation of the earlier, still partially hidden, love of a trustworthy God.[22] "Truth" here denotes: conveyed judgment truth or token of the veracity of Him who spoke this Judgment in the world. One needs to distinguish here first of all between the divine and human use of judgment truth. Then also [between] truth in the theory of judgment and truth in the theory of knowledge. The former presupposes the latter, but not vice versa.

(§50) *Logos*-speculation forgot first of all to draw the principal boundary between God and creature. That it also did not pay attention to the difference between the theory of judgment and the theory of knowledge speaks for itself given its dependence on antiquity.

---

21   A. Kuyper, *E Voto Dordraceno, Toelichting op den Heidelbergschen Catechismus*, I (Amsterdam, Pretoria, Potchefstroom: Höveker en Wormser, 1904), 320.

22   For more in this line see Th. Zahn, *Das Evangelium des Johannes*, 3rd and 4th ed. (Leipzig: Deichert, 1912), 555. [The distinction between partial and full revelation of the truth is in step with the orders of the Old and New Testament respectively; A.T.]

(§51) The errors of Origen derive from those of Philo. As for the epistemological errors I mention merely that, instead of distinguishing between the Holy Scripture's anthropomorphic communication about God's activity and its no-longer-anthropomorphic communication about the cosmos, he introduces the entirely different threefold distinction between its historico-dogmatic, psycho-moral, and pneumatical [i.e., spiritual] sense. Then there is also the humanizing of the divine Logos.

(§52) Tertullian and Lactantius took a different position, one more oriented to the Stoics. This enabled them to derive arguments from the sense-perceptual context of knowledge in favor of a skepticism that, in a negative sense, was supposed to support the faith.

(§53) Accordingly, those active in epistemology at this time should be sought for the most part among the heathen Neoplatonists. [/19] On the basis of their psychology they ventured a novel connection of the subject-object schema with the pyramid structure of the form-matter metaphysics. In brief, their main thought is as follows. Everything flows forth from the One; which is no longer self-consciousness, but something even more elevated than that. Of what emanates in different degrees of reality from the One, the first place is occupied by the intellect [*geest*], which accommodates within itself, as self-consciousness, the duality of subject and object. The subjective [factor] is characteristically active, the objective is its content. In this way the act-content schema crosses that of the form-material in the human being. Act and form touch each other, material and content lie at the opposite ends of the two crossing lines.

(§54) Now as to the latter [i.e., matter and content in this constellation], this involves a break in epistemology with the theory of abstraction, even though this [theory] is taken to the limit in metaphysics. In the former [i.e., act and form] there is already gain. But there is more: for it also counts as an advantage that self-consciousness is divested of its Aristotelian apotheosis on the basis of the correct realization that no further distinctions are allowed in a primal unity. However, on the debit side, the identification of The One with God silences all theology.

(§55) A third advantage can be noted as well. The emphasis now falls for the first time on the *forming* of concepts.♦ But also here multiple disadvantages counterbalance this gain. By equating form and act[23] the nature of form becomes active, something that it does not deserve, for

---

23   Cf. Plotinus, *Enneades*, 2, 4, 4, S.105, cited in Ueberweg-Praechter, *Grundrisz der Geschichte der Philosophie des Altertums* (Berlin: Mittler, 1920), 630.

this is proper only for the subject who wields the form as organon. The correlation of *noesis* and *hyle noetike* – in modern terms: [intellectual] act and [intellectual] content – can only be understood on the basis of this identification of form and forming. But precisely for this reason it should be rejected as erroneous. The activity of the soul aims at the combination of form and content; the correlate of this activity is thus not the content but the organon, the instrument, and this is not itself active. The logical form is no more immanent in the mind [*geest*] than is the content. And finally, here too we must challenge the view that "knowing of" ["*weten van*"] and that about which there is this knowing are pre-figurations of the subject-object schema. This view brings the Neoplatonists to accept, as do many in our day as well, a mind-immanent epistemological object.

(§56) In Aurelius Augustine we encounter a world of thought that is, in part, completely different, at least insofar as we focus on the ripe fruit that his life offers us. After Stoic philosophy had driven him into the arms of the Manicheans, Augustine, still under the influence of the Academy's skepticism, came to question the Manichean identification of moral good and evil with light and darkness. He was subsequently able to wrestle himself free of this skepticism, which sought happiness in abandoning the longing for certainty, only through the support of Neoplatonism, which had influenced the exegetical work of his confessor, Ambrose, to be as symbol-laden as that of Origen.[24] [/20]

(§57) And this framework [of Neoplatonism] had a lasting effect on Augustine, even though its influence diminishes in his life as he came to be the positive theologian of predestination.[25] That comes as no surprise because whoever acknowledges, on the basis of Holy Scripture, a God who elects and governs all according to his Counsel can in the long run have no peace with a theory that springs from an entirely different seedbed.

(§58) In the meantime, the older he became the more the needs of the church laid a claim on him. His theory of knowledge, which indeed has

---

24 Augustine, *Confessiones* [Book] 5, [Chapter] 14.

25 Th.L. Haitjema, *Augustinus' Wetenschapsidee, Bijdrage tot de kennis van de opkomst der idee eener Christelijke wetenschap in de antieke wereld* (Utrecht: Drukkerij De Industrie, J. van Druten, 1917), 99–104. (Dissertation)

♦ [This is central to "*ratio*," i.e., the problem of rationality. "*Ratio*" involves the logical form in use, hence it also calls for a subject who, in a properly specified role, "wields the form as an organon"; A.T.]

commendable features, still displays numerous traces of the framework that had eased his transition to Christianity. That is why there is more to take issue with here than one might initially expect in light of his prefiguring a number of thoughts that are indeed Calvinistic.

(§59) Neoplatonic influence is behind both the one-sided treatment of truth, preferably from the point of view of values, and its neglect in favor of matters aesthetic. But the spirit of antiquity is also clearly noticeable in the fundamental thesis that philosophy is practiced from an urge for happiness.[26] The same background is evident in many epistemological expressions. God includes the world of ideas; accordingly, the subject, participating in this world, ascends to Him in love of Him, the highest good. Hence, what he reproaches philosophers for is not their speculating about a gradually diminishing reality – something he himself is guilty of – but only for the arrogance that fancies that this knowledge can be acquired without God's help and completely disconnected from the Christian church.[27] For him the inner opposition between humanism and Christianity is cancelled by the conversion that lets love dominate over knowledge and that acknowledges the authority of the ecclesiastical community. But he failed to notice that knowledge itself is structured in a way different than was taught by Iamblichus and Porphyry.[28] So too he fails to discover the danger of equating "knowing that" and "knowing of"; raising the latter again to the starting point of his view of knowledge.[29]

(§60) Naturally the consequence is that on the one hand a psychical – not psychological! – moment [i.e., "knowing of"] is wrongfully called "true"; on the other hand in this way much that deserves the name "true" remains open to doubt. He attempts to free himself from this impasse in two ways: in part by accepting innate concepts[30] – *inter alia* those of point, line, and plane[31] – and in part by calling on the help of faith. One ought to believe not only one's own origin, but also the existence of the soul of fellow-creatures and that of bodies.[32]

In other words, to believe, according to Augustine, is not a matter

---

26   Augustine, *Contra Academicos* [Book] 1, [Chapter] 2.

27   Augustine, *Confessiones* [Book] 7, [Chapter] 9.

28   E. Troeltsch, *Augustin, die Christliche Antike und das Mittelalter* (München und Berlin: Oldenbourg, 1915), 116–123.

29   Augustine, *Soliloquia* [Book] 2, 1.

30   Augustine, *Confessiones* [Book] 10, [Chapter] 12.

31   Augustine, *De quantitate animae*, Chapters 12 and 13.

32   Augustine, *Confessiones* [Book] 6, [Chapter] 5.

of believing *in* God who communicates truth about His works, a trusting that is fed continually by believing that it is or was as He says. For this includes believing that everything in the cosmos happens under the law and according to distinct laws, which in turn stimulates inquiry, initiated in faithful obedience, into the laws that hold for [/21] each domain.

No, faith [for Augustine] only has a secondary, auxiliary role, namely it is called upon to complement that which is evidently initially hostile to that faith. Yes, sometimes the *ratio* even takes the lead in guiding faith, which is not surprising when the *logos*, on which also rests what God has revealed, is confused with our concept formation and the principles that hold for this.[33] Time and again then Augustine wanders off toward a speculation that erases the principal boundary that lies between God and the cosmos; when that happens God for him coincides with the truth and the truth, the light above him, becomes God to him. Linked to this is that the first thing asked of the believer is not obedience, but purity and holiness: those near unto God intuit the truth by means of the soul, which remains the organ of divine experience.[34] Entirely in the same vein, when characterizing the difference between truths conveyed to him by others, but never fully grasped, and truths one comes to possess through one's own effort, he replaces the latter with knowledge brought forth from within.[35] In that way the discovery of many depth dimensions within the life of the soul, of which he may be justly proud, led him to exaggerate his break with Neoplatonism, which he actually never really overcame.

(§61) However, do not forget one thing. Precisely because consciousness and truth still lie intertwined, there is, after all, more than just naive

---

33 *S. Aureli Augustini Hipponiensis episcope epistulae. Recensuit et commentario critico instruxit* Al. Goldbacher, Pars I, Pragae-Vindobonae-Lipsiae, F. Tempski, 1895, Ep. 120, 3, 706–707 [Latin quotation in translation]: "And so, the prophet stated quite reasonably, *Unless you believe, you will not understand* (Is. 7:9 LXX). There he undoubtedly distinguished these two and gave the counsel that we should believe first in order that we may be able to understand what we believe. Hence it was reasonably commanded that faith should precede reason. For, if this command is not reasonable it is, therefore, unreasonable. Heaven forbid! If, then, it is reasonable that faith precede reason with respect to certain great truths that cannot yet be grasped, however slight the reason is that persuades us to this, it undoubtedly also comes before faith." [Augustine, "Letter to Consentius" Letter 120; from: *The Works of Saint Augustine* (3rd Release). Electronic edition. Edition Information. Past Masters Preface (Charlottesville, Virginia, USA: InteLex Corporation, 2001), volume II, 2. 131.]

34 J. Bernhart, *Die philosophische Mystik des Mittelalters* (München: Reinhardt, 1922), 53–60.

35 Augustine, *Confessiones* [Book] 7, [Chapter] 20.

psychologism in this theory of "knowing" [*weten*] – although its presence cannot be denied. E.g., in Augustine the thought already occurs of God's arrangements. When viewed [*geschouwd*] by the mind, such a terrain (for psychical reality)[36] exhibits some traces of agreement with a circle of consideration [*gezichtsveld*], and this viewing indeed resembles somewhat the peculiarity of the intuition.[37] We note, as being distinctly typical, that for all sense impressions, also when they are deceptive with respect to the knowledge regarding the outer world, the reality, in particular the psychical reality, is emphatically maintained.[38]

D. *The Middle Ages*

(§62) The Middle Ages never let this gain [of a realist psychology] slip away entirely. For that matter, also in other areas it offers more insight than is commonly thought. And this could hardly be otherwise. European life, now Christianized – even if only superficially – posed entirely new questions and placed the tradition of antiquity in a new light. For the proper evaluation of this period, one ought not forget, certainly not in our [Reformed] circle, that the contempt that later befell it arose in the main from an all-dominating difference in lifestyle that reduced interest in the questions that scholasticism addressed to zero. Most everyone who denies divine revelation will shrug at its efforts, perhaps with bemused pity. And even those who avoid this error but fail to acknowledge the moment of truth in this revelation will also find the endeavor of scholasticism strange.

(§63) Yet anyone who considers all this and seriously takes it into account can hardly call the meditations of Christians in those days Christian thought. [/22] For the nature of the work is determined not only by what one hopes to achieve, but more so by the foundation on which one stands. And this [foundation] was sought in the philosophy of antiquity,

---

36 H. Eibl, *Augustin und die Patristik* (München: Reinhardt, 1923), 300. [In the copy text, the three words here bracketed – in Dutch: "voor het psychische." – occur at the end of the current paragraph, unattached to the prior sentence but with footnote number "38." This is probably meant to be a textual addition, but it wasn't carried out. On careful consideration, the current position is its most likely intended destination, all the more so since the footnote reference to Eibl concerns psychology and understanding the Trinity in Augustine. The footnote numbers of this paragraph have had to be adjusted to retain a linear order (footnote "38" now being numbered "36"). The round brackets around the phrase are not in the copy text. A.T.]

37 Augustine, *Confessiones* [Book] 7, [Chapter] 10.

38 Augustine, *Contra Academicos*, [Book] 3, [Chapters] 11–12 and 26.

sometimes in a more Platonizing direction, at other times with a strong Aristotelian inclination. But precisely for that reason, given our earlier critique, we are convinced a priori that the well-intended attempt to do justice to revelation was doomed to fail.

(§64) I want to support this assertion more specifically, insofar as it concerns epistemology, by focusing on the dispute about the reality of universals, the theories as to how knowledge arises, and finally statements about the relation of faith and knowledge [geloof en weten].

1. The reality of universals

(§65) As to the universals – even though one must agree with A. Dempf that the dispute that arose on this point is, historically speaking, only one part of the differences concerning the concept of substance,[39] discussing this topic must take precedence here because, considered epistemologically, it is one of the most indisputable proofs for the claim that very many difficulties at this time are rooted in a trust in ancient philosophy, which, itself in confusion, did not appear to be able to answer the new questions in a satisfactory fashion. And when clarity is lacking, dispute arises.

(§66) The confusion in Greek thought, already signaled above, consisted in the rather ambiguous use of the term "general." They took it to mean both the relation of a truth to that about which it holds, and the repeatedly recurring identical moments in different concepts. This is the case for Plato as well as for Aristotle. But when reflecting more specifically on the foundation they part ways. In Plato it is ideas that are general, characterized by their independence – in the sense of their being disconnected from individual things – and by their higher place in the order of the pyramid structure.

Now the realm of truth is indeed independent insofar as it [truth] is truth through nothing but its own character. But it ought never to be taken as disconnected from what is non-logical. For all truth is truth about something. Now as to the apriority of truth, the pyramid image should be abandoned entirely, on grounds explained above. In an order-theoretical sense, however, the *logical* is indeed the lowest sphere, which explains how it is that all the [other] independent law-spheres rest on the logical [sphere] and display its analogy. In that sense, it is the analogy of the logical [in non-logical spheres], and not the logical itself [it being

---

39 Alois Dempf, *Die Hauptform mittelalterlicher Weltanschauung* (München und Berlin: Oldenbourg, 1925), 74.

a distinct sphere], that has universal significance, also independently of knowledge. And since we can compare the creation of the law-spheres to the writing of a well-organized book, in which the later chapters build on the content of the earlier ones, one may even conclude to there being an apriority *in mente Dei* [in the mind of God].

But Plato's followers did not always distinguish so well. E.g., they confused the logical [law-sphere] in the cosmos with the *logos* in God's plan, and even adopted [from the latter] the schema [/23] of thought; although in the end this schema, the [logical] form, was sought in the human mind.

But that was not the end of it. The logical [factor] is not the same as truth; truth is the analogy of the logical in the non-logical, for truth is always *about* [something]. Now there are two ways in which such a truth can come to be in one's possession: first of all by viewing [*schouwen*] a circle of consideration [*gezichtsveld*], i.e., by viewing the modally determined analogy as such [that is implicit in it]; secondly by using the logical schema as organon for tracing specific analogies of the logical in the circle of consideration that is in itself not logical, thereby turning that circle into a field of inquiry [*gedachtenveld*]. This [second way] is how concepts arise. ◆

Once concepts are formed these provisionally acquired results can be compared. Doing so makes clear that identical moments of truth constantly recur in different concepts; moments which in that sense may be typified as general – over against the non-recurring ones as special. But *logos* and grasped truth were not kept sufficiently distinct, which is why misunderstanding arose and dispute was inevitable. The realist adage "*universale ante rem*" [universals prior to things] is entirely correct provided one takes the *universale* as pertaining to the logical. But it becomes meaningless when applied to recurrent moments of grasped truth about

---

◆[Here we see that the *logos* involves the cosmic order, i.e., the *logos* itself as a distinct logical law-sphere (or circle of consideration), and the analogies of this law-sphere in the non-logical law-spheres resting on it and as modified by these law-spheres. Discerning this in the cosmic order yields (metaphysical) intuitions of judgments of discerning. The discerning (or viewing) of the logical law-sphere itself offers the opportunity of grasping the "logical form." The latter is the schema of a relational structure, this being a system, *modally* qualified, of *terms* standing in a *relation*. The form is used by the subject to trace more specific relational patterns in the states of affairs of a non-logical law-sphere. Rational insight (*ratio*, or concept formation) is based on this use of the logical schema. Truth is presupposed in connection with both *logos* and *ratio*. A.T.]

something; for then one can get no further than the *"veritas non sine re"* [no truth without things].

(§67) This criticism pertains only to the *universale*. It is not cancelled but actually becomes weightier when also focusing on *res* [thing]. For the extreme realists of the Middle Ages the universals are evidently not themselves *res*, for otherwise the expression *"universale ante rem"* loses its meaning. Despite this shibboleth's Platonic look, it actually implies an Aristotelian thing-concept: a thing is the individual that, other than its appearing, is at the same time material for a more general form. "Thing" is understood here to be "appearing essence." Thus essence and object of perception stand to each other as the inner and the outer [respectively], as the hidden psyche of the fellow human being to his/her visible body. But thing, either as object of perception or as an essence in the sense of a cosmic unity [e.g., an individual], is [only] useful in metaphysics. If one refers to a thing in a special science, then all that is relevant is the intersection in the cosmic unity applied according to the law of the circle of consideration; i.e., the something that in connection with concept formation first becomes a moment and then a system, within which [when analyzed] sub-moments are distinguished.

(§68) It should be noted that scholasticism did not itself raise this criticism – "thing" remained individual perceptible essence. No wonder that logic, lacking the character of truth that only the concept can ennoble, regressed to language psychology. What is perceived is named with words, and what one asserts of it is expressed in a sentence. The theory of John Roscelin – one reminiscent of the Stoics – emphasized named words, while Peter Abelard's psychologically more elevated *sermo*-theory [speech theory] let the emphasis fall more on the asserted sentence. (Abelard's *sermo*-theory, by the way, was more important for introducing changes in pedagogy [/24] than for transforming the method of research.[40]) As for "moments of truth": similarity was diverted to the psychical [level], identity to the *res*, but the identity in that which was similar, the *identitas momenti veritatis non per mentem* [the identity of the moment of truth is not through the mind], fell from view.

(§69) One needs only compare the summary of these two statements, *"veritas non sine re"* [§66] and *"identitas momenti veritatis non per mentem"* [§68], with Thomas' realism to realize how half-hearted he was. Which is to say: he settled the endless struggle between realism and nominalism – itself the result of a lack of distinctions – by combining

---

40 Dempf, *Die Hauptform mittelalterlicher Weltanschauung*, 90 ff.

the following two basic claims: "the separate is the true substance" and "the general arises by means of the subjective activity of the mind." But this is a solution only in appearance. For, as regards the first statement, a substance is either an essence [per se] – but that is no help to the special sciences because epistemologically speaking this cosmic unity is but a moment or a system [of moments] only for metaphysics – or it is a perceptible essence, with its principle of individuation in matter.[41] But then the whole problem is again reduced to the relationship between essence and appearance, and the special sciences are still bereft of the *something* about which they are to inquire. And although the second statement appears to have greater epistemological value than the first, in that it proceeds from perception's value in connection with knowing, it actually robs knowledge of its truth character, and in so doing makes an important concession to nominalism.

2.   *How knowledge arises*
(§70) This discussion leads automatically to the second problem, namely *the origin of knowledge*. Common to all is the subject-medium schema, the assumption that the medium affects the subject, and that the subject assimilates perceptual content through its inborn concepts. For the rest there are again differences.

(§71) There are first of all the followers of Augustine. In Neoplatonic fashion they relate subject and object to each other as (active) form to its content. Thus the sense-organs include, potentially, the sensorial forms, which, when stimulated by the sense-impressions, lead to sensorial knowledge. A similar situation holds between mind and intelligible object in connection with the acquisition of non-sensorial knowledge. Sensorial knowledge and non-sensorial knowledge are parallel: the latter finds its occasion, not its ground, in the former; which is why the Aristotelian bifurcation of the *nous* also falls away. Through God there is knowledge of what is non-sensorial. He discloses to us both the terrain of morality and the region that is accessible only in fever and hallucinations! The unity of knowledge and of truth is here sacrificed for the supposed duality of those terrains about which knowledge includes truth. The act-content schema holds sway. Instead of analyzing further – which this approach has made practically impossible – one retreats again to heathen metaphysics, claiming that its theory of the essential similarity between [/25] it and God is equivalent to the teaching of the image of God (even

---

41   B. Hauréau, *Histoire de la Philosophie scolastique*, II, 1 (Paris: Pedone Lauriel, 1880), 350 ff.

though in the Holy Scripture the latter is never considered apart from the covenant of God with humankind).

(§72) This [Augustinian] approach, represented quite faithfully[42] *inter alia* by William of Auvergne, differs appreciably from the Aristotelian one represented by Thomas Aquinas. The horizontal correlation of form and content makes way for the vertical of form and matter. Sensorial knowledge makes way for knowledge that arises through abstraction: the *imaginatio* abstracts from the *sensus*, and the *intellectus*, which has an active and a passive part, abstracts from the *imaginatio*. The *intellectus agens* [the active intellect] includes certain inborn principles that allows it penetrate to the *quiddity* [whatness] of things; *intelligere* is *intus-legere* [to understand is to collect within]. Truth is *adaequatio* [being adequate to; agreement]; knowledge is the *"adaequatio intellectus et rei"* ["agreement of thought and thing"]. Knowledge shifts from possessing truth to being a certain form of truth, acquired through adaptation to the nature of things as mediated by the *phantasmata* [images of the imagination]. The things are then said to be intentionally present to mind.[43]

(§73) Further removed from Aristotle is the older Franciscan school. They maintained that more is inborn than the psychologized logical form; they also introduced content from non-logical regions, e.g., the so-called eternal truths of mathematics.[44] Hence here again the pyramid structure occasions a pantheistic blurring of the boundaries between the eternity of God and the nature of a circle of consideration where time plays no role [e.g., number and space]. At the same time one can see here the consequences of introducing an incision [between the non-temporal mathematical spheres and the other temporal spheres] that is totally strange to epistemology; since number cannot be included under essence nor appearing, it was simply placed in the subject!

3. *The relation of faith and knowledge*
(§74) Finally, there is the problem of *believing* that, and *knowing that* in a scientific sense.

---

42   Ueberweg-Baumgartner, *Grundriss der Geschichte der Philosophie der patristischen und scholastischen Zeit*, 10th ed. (Berlin: Mittler, 1915), 418–420.

43   J.M. Verweyen, *Die Philosophie des Mittelalters* (Berlin und Leipzig: De Gruyter & Co., 1921), 135–139, especially 139, note 2.

44   Ueberweg-Baumgartner, *Grundriss der Geschichte der Philosophie der patristischen und scholastischen Zeit*, 431–452.

(§75) As *inter alia* J. Woltjer explicitly notes,[45] *believing that* [*geloven dat*] and *knowing that* [*weten dat*] have in common the moment of subjective certainty. But they differ too: "believing that" expresses the assumption of a communication coming from someone else; "knowing that" does not exclude such a communication, but it tends to disregard this. Hence, in everyday language, and not only in Holy Scripture, "believing that" and "knowing that" are used interchangeably when the person who conveyed what is believed is deemed trustworthy. "Knowing that" does not exclude communication, but neither does it require it. "Knowing that" can arise through believing a dependable communication as well as through one's own inquiry, when using the dependable method of intuition and concept formation.

(§76) One should, however, make a sharp distinction – though not a separation – between "believing that" [*geloven dat*] and "believing in" [*geloven in*]. Precise language usage limits "believe in" to those cases in which an expectation of salvation figures; e.g., "The soldiers of Napoleon believed in their general." The Christian therefore prefers not to use this word [/26] otherwise than in connection with the ground of one's expectation of salvation, namely with God. For "believing *in* God" is different from "believing *that* He exists," though of course the latter is presupposed in the former, at least if such believing is not to be reduced to the level of autosuggestion. "*Believing that*" refers first of all to a discerning of something on the basis of a communication made about this something by someone else, and secondly to grasping more deeply what is conveyed with the help, say, of science.

(§77) The following is a short summary in connection with the relationship of religion and theology.

"Believing in" expresses the fact that regeneration, progressing in a continuous process, is linked to an awareness of being called to *well-being* or *blessedness* [*heil of zaligheid*]. "Believing that" expresses confidence in the one who communicates. That could be God himself or also one of the means that he uses for this purpose. In this sense one can speak of a direct and an indirect communication. But both cases concern communication, thus they concern a word spoken by him in the covenant with humankind. That is why the distinction of direct and indirect communication is not co-terminus with that of revelation through His word and through His work; it falls entirely within the context of the word revelation. The latter presupposes the covenant that God one-sidedly ini-

---

45   J. Woltjer, *De zekerheid der wetenschap* (Amsterdam: Van Schaïk, 1907), 7–10.

tiated with humankind, but which, after being instituted, has of course a two-sided character. By virtue of the creation of the disposition to this covenant, the human being is said to be created according to God's image. The communication in words may therefore be called revelation, for it informs about what otherwise would remain hidden, in other words, about God and the relationship of the creatures to him.

In this connection two remarks are in order. In the first place, this communication takes place in the covenant, thus always *under* the law. God speaks in what for the human being is understandable language and words; hence it is inappropriate for us to attempt to translate this communication into the form that it has for God, or [to display] humility when such an attempt fails. And in the second place, this word revelation speaks about him – which includes communication about his relationship to creatures – and about the relationship of creatures to him. *That is why* the word revelation – the direct, but of course in imitation of it also the indirect – always treats creatures as *cosmic unities* or speaks about them in the language of everyday perception. Science only comes into the picture as one of the *tasks* to which the human being is called, and this call to [fulfill] a task follows upon being called to well-being [*heil*].

An important note in this context is that a decisive change in the relationship of creatures to God came about in history through the fall; in that connection an important moment was added to the word revelation in Paradise, namely that of grace. This grace does not hold for all persons, which is why it is called "special grace," and yet is so prominent – it being postlapsarian and, given our fear, well-nigh incredible – that all the rest, though none of it is deleted, recedes to the background for its sake.

(§78) These distinctions intend in no way to exhaust this rich topic. [/27] They offer no more than what is minimally necessary to illuminate scholasticism's faulty solutions to poorly posed problems.

(§79) Here too the Middle Ages appear to be anything but uniform. The Augustinian approach sees things so entirely different than the followers of Thomas Aquinas.

a. *Augustinian trend*
(§80) As for the Augustinian approach, the bifurcation of knowledge adopted from the Neoplatonists allows one in the knowledge of the a priori world of ideas to view a good that leads to God, the top of the pyramid. While Augustine did not challenge this design, he did insist that the pride of philosophers who delude themselves in attributing this knowl-

edge to themselves needs to be replaced by humility and the spirit of love that reigns in the church of Christ.[46] But even if one maintains that these revisions are quite simply fruits of regeneration [*levendmaking*], one in no way does justice to believing the communication, extended over the course of time, about how God's relationship to humankind changed with the course of events. Given antiquity's lack of historical awareness one can hardly expect that their systems would include sufficient distinctions in this regard. Theology's connecting with antiquity entailed for it a lack of all independence over against philosophy – and what a philosophy!

(§81) What was good in Augustine, particularly the distinction of humankind in two groups, was almost lost with the conversion of the German people groups. For now, in universalistic-popish fashion, humankind was put on a par with the church in general. Thus a place had to be prepared for it as well in the pyramid. Quite obviously, the rank proper to it was between God and nature, i.e., everything else. Thus while her connection with grace and reconciliation – and thus with a specific period of human history – was on the one hand maintained as firmly as possible, she nevertheless still appeared as an eternal component in the pan-teleological system.[47] Although this standpoint brought theology gain in that a distinct terrain was vindicated for her, this advantage was only allotted her at the cost of a courtly bow to a philosophy that misunderstood what was most important to her.

(§82) In addition, the parallelism of subject and object – both of which had to submit to the same metaphysical schema – brought with it that this supernatural world was linked to an equally supernatural organ, namely faith. Yet, when the Middle Ages confused existence judgment (in our sense of the term) with the judgment of perception and its analogy, insufficient attention was given to the moment of [pistical] discerning when it came to the word revelation of God. Hence while, on the one hand, regeneration and "believing in" [*geloven in*] were ecclesiasticized [*verkerkelijkt*],[48] "believing that" [*geloven dat*] was limited to the formation of concepts about this supernatural domain, differing only in degree from the activity in the field of theology. [/28]

(§83) The first consequence naturally was that the value of the last named

---

46   Troeltsch, *Augustin, die Christliche Antike und das Mittelalter,* 119.

47   H. Bavinck, *Gereformeerde Dogmatiek* I, 2nd ed. (Kampen: Kok, 1906), 374.

48   Kuyper, *E Voto Dordraceno, Toelichting op den Heidelbergschen Catechismus,* III (Amsterdam, Pretoria, Potchefstroom: Höveker en Wormser, 1904), 396 ff.

science [i.e., theology] was grossly exaggerated, for which it would later be doubly penalized. For when it was discovered that this discipline wanted to be more than merely a science, it stood exposed to justified criticism on the part of those for whom genuine faith was primary, but no less so for those concerned about the purity of science.

(§84) The second consequence was that "believing that" became attributed to a higher understanding, namely the epistemologically construed theory of the *donum superadditum* [superadded gift]. Thus it did not remain the ubiquitous acceptance of a dependable communication, i.e., a communication from God about an Essence [*Wezen*] [i.e., Himself] and a relation about which only He can inform us. And also the awareness of being indirect lost significance, namely the beatific believing, in inseparable faith regarding the history of revelation and the dependability of the media, was leveled to an acceptance of the historical [reality] about which the Holy Scripture, among other things, informs us.

b. *Other trends*

(§85) What did the connection between "believing that" and "knowing that" look like at the height of scholasticism, when Augustine's more rationalistic standpoint was provisionally overcome? In answering this question one can distinguish, with J.M. Verweyen,[49] a semi-rationalistic and an anti-rationalistic approach.

(§86) The semi-rationalistic approach in the history of Christian thought is studded with such reputable names as Anselm of Canterbury and Thomas Aquinas. For Anselm, the author of *Proslogion* and *Cur Deus Homo*, understanding and faith have, from the start, a teleological connection: inquiry forms the foundation of faith – which is different from what the well-known "*credo ut intelligam*" ["I believe in order that I may understand"] might suggest. Reason must review, according to Anselm, the fact of revelation so as to prepare belief for the revealed content. A kind of existence judgment precedes concept formation here, but not as judgment of the intuition of the [pistical] modality; rather this judgment is placed in a lower sphere analogous to the relation between perception and thought in the natural [realm]. To theology is then entrusted the assimilation of what is accepted through awareness. The danger does not lie there so much as elsewhere: believing the communication furnished on God's command about divine revelation was in principle [*in beginsel*] supplanted by the demand for an inquiry that is *not bound to*

---

49   Verweyen, *Die Philosophie des Mittelalters,* 112–134.

faith, whose scope is expressed in the question: "Has God communicated something?" In this way the "*intellige ut credas*" ["understand in order to believe"] precedes, already with Anselm, the "*credo ut intelligam.*"[50]

(§87) Thomas attempts to offer more of an analysis of the distinct character of faith. He recognizes, as does Anselm, something of the difference between communicated truth and truth found through applying oneself, but he fails to see the difference between the regions about which God and human beings communicate. Further inquiry [on Thomas' part] does make him sense that, when it comes to communicated truth, one both accepts the truth and [/29] trusts the veracity of the communicator. Both are indissolubly connected: veracity is not the same as love of truth, [rather] it is a being bound to truth, a not being *able* to speak any untruth, not now or ever.

Now "applying oneself" and "accepting" are not as such theoretical attitudes. However, if I focus directly – thus without communication – on understanding truth, then what I stand over against is neither human nor anything analogous to being human. I stand over against "truth." But when truth is communicated other factors play a role; e.g., the veracity of the communicator is for me the warrant for the truth of what I myself have not investigated or cannot investigate. Precisely this factor occasions, in these circumstances, that my willing no longer needs to be focused on the effort of inquiry but rather on apprehending, through listening or reading, [what is conveyed]. Hence willing is a factor that is present in every acquisition of truth. But applying oneself and listening is as such no longer a willing. And the truth has altogether nothing more to do with willing, whether this concerns truth about a cosmic connection or a trans-cosmic one.

However Thomas confuses assenting with willing. First of all he equates my making a judgment (compare *assentire* [agreeing] with *sententia* [opinion, decision]) that is in agreement with the judgment of the communicator in which his knowledge – and thus my future knowledge – is contained, with my accepting that knowledge. Hence for him to confess is the same as to believe. Secondly he looks for a difference within the subject that is analogous to the difference between trans-cosmic and cosmic connection. Thereby he fails to see that truth always remains truth, and that "believing that" is only the psychical correlate of the *communication* that replaces the inquiry of the one listening, but that it doesn't replace a specific region about which the communicated truth enlightens.

---

50   Verweyen, *Die Philosophie des Mittelalters*, 113.

Hence "believing that" is not correlate with a specific region but correlate with a specific manner of knowledge acquisition.

That behind believing God's truth lies also the change of the whole person, of one's interests, and thus also of one's willing is something completely different. Through sin interest in anything that has to do with God has come to pine and die. If the human being is ever going to be able to listen again, that interest has to first awaken and thereby reorient the human being to a willingness to listen. But these givens of Holy Scripture offer no grounds for equating this listening acceptance with willing; and even less so, in addition, to identify it with confessing.

(§88) I can't take leave of this [semi-rationalistic] group without briefly recalling how living by the tradition dictated the fencing off of the "supernatural" region over against the natural. Research on their part was not totally absent, but it took place wholly in the spirit of Aristotle. Thomas dedicated a great part of his life to writing commentaries on him. As a result, subjective faith and reason and objective church and world [/30] came to stand as the spirit of Holy Scripture to that of Aristotle's writings. This made it relatively easy to make out what portion of the content of the former [i.e., Scripture] could [also] be discovered by reason [alone]. (i) To the latter belonged everything found in the Greek philosopher on which the Bible was silent. (ii) If, on the contrary, the Holy Scripture spoke of something not to be found in Aristotle, then it was certain that this transcended reason. (iii) Where both sources were completely congruent then one spoke of a "theorem," to be proven by the strong and to be believed by those with weaker mental capacities. (iv) If they were only partially congruent, then the dogma based on it was a mixture. For example, the creation of the world can be proven, [but] that it was not eternal had to be believed. Keep in mind, in connection with the last two cases, that owing to a lack of historical awareness much was attributed to Aristotle that he never asserted. For example, the proof of the creation [of the world] was acquired by equating creation with the emanation of all that is out of the universal cause.[51] (v) If the two sources contradicted each other, then the old wisdom had to be sacrificed, what Thomas experienced as a *sacrificium intellectus* [sacrifice of the intellect].

(§89) When the boundary between theology and the other sciences is drawn in this way, the evident conclusion is that because what theology deals with has practical meaning it can no longer be called a "science" in the strict sense of the word. [This leads to an anti-rationalist approach;

51 Verweyen, *Die Philosophie des Mittelalters*, 122.

cf. §85.] That at least is what Duns Scotus concluded – despite his maintaining that faith is "safer" [to bank on] than knowing [*weten*]. When the latter was emphasized more, one soon lapsed into disdaining science from a desire for [faith's] certainty. Those who rob theology of its purely scientific character and yet, confusing it with religion, still assume it to embrace everything are forced to value the search for and the finding of all truth – however acquired – less than those who, honoring theology as a science, realize that theology deserves an independent (though not unbounded) terrain, and refuse to pay for the acknowledgement of its value by excluding it from the *universitas scientiarum* [the totality of the sciences]. The humiliation of science so as to elevate faith is an unavoidable consequence of all rationalism generally. It wasn't absent in the Middle Ages either, as evidenced by, say, Peter Damian in the receptive period and exemplified by someone like John of Jandun during the waning of scholasticism.

(§90) And yet, however dangerous this skepticism might have been, one ought not to forget that at the time it could often offer a refuge for the deeper insight that there was animosity between the spirit of Aristotle – who, soon removed of a Christian veneer, will be among those dominating the Renaissance[52] – and that of Christ.

(§91) That said, distinguishing skepticism and this insight is important, particularly with an eye to a proper understanding of the differences between the chief proponents of the Reformation.

E. *The Reformation*

(§92) Mysticism too often did not see the regeneration, and the awakening of interest, that is behind faith. But it did discover early [/31] on that faith involves acceptance, and that for a Christian more is to be accepted than merely truth. Now one could deny expecting to find any such moment of truth in these "treasures of Christ," but this is not the case along the line leading to the Reformation. What one does find is the neglect of the difference between God's revelation to the prophets and their communication to the members of the Church, i.e., between word-revelation and Scripture-revelation. In this way, although the moment of truth in the revelation is not denied, it nevertheless remains very limited in its extent. And what one "hears (personally)" is then often considered to be

---

52 W. Goetz, "Die Wiederaufname der Antike im Mittelalter und in der Renaissance," in *Vom Altertum zur Gegenwart, Die Kulturzusammenhänge in den Hauptepochen und auf den Hauptgebieten* , 2nd ed. (Leipzig und Berlin: Teubner, 1921), 49–61, specially 56.

of equal value to the hearing of the prophets. In this way people lost the link to the history of revelation.

(§93) In this manner the Roman Catholic distinction of the divine and human *factor* in religion could be cancelled, as in Martin Luther. But for a deeper analysis of faith this mysticism offered considerably less than what Luther himself thought was necessary – witness his debate with Desiderius Erasmus on the method of exegesis.[53] That said, he would not be the one to offer this analysis, hindered as he was by his anthropological point of departure. For knowledge too can only be approached aright when viewed from a higher standpoint.

(§94) Which was precisely John Calvin's forte. He too was in no way a professional epistemologist. On the contrary, what is so beneficent about him, and in light of his well-known link with Augustine doubly to be appreciated, is precisely that he is fully a theologian. His aversion to mixing theology with philosophy brought him, much more so than in Luther's case, to lay a close connection between the formal and the material principle of theology. Calvin shared the German reformer's regard for the formal principle, but when it came to the material principle he totally went his own way. This was required in order to be consequential. For with regard to salvation [*zaligheid*] through faith Luther took his point of departure in anthropology, and thus stopped doing purely theological work even before he had good and well begun. In Calvin's way of thinking it is God who is "in the beginning." He is the Creator of everything through His will. That is why the cosmos is merely His project [*werkstuk*]. He can treat it as He pleases, [and] reveal Himself in it in special ways. But then it is the Infinite that grasps the finite, and the contrary is never the case: "*finitum non est capax infiniti*" ["The finite is not able to grasp the infinite"]. This statement dominates the Christology[54] as well as the theory of the sacraments and that of well-being [*heil*].

(§95) But precisely in his seeing so clearly the boundary between Him who posits laws and they that are subject to them, he was also able to demarcate things sharply elsewhere. First of all, the theory of predestination brought him to a definite break with the scholastics' equating of

---

53 E. Katzer, *Luther und Kant. Ein Beitrag zur innern Entwicklungsgeschichte* [/73] *des deutschen Protestantismus* (Giessen: Töpelmann, 1910), 23 ff.

54 To my amazement Georg Lasson forgets this when he asks – in *Kant-Studien* 30 (1925): 198 – in connection with my earlier defense of this statement: "Can this be consistent with the fundamental teaching of Christianity, the incarnation of God and the Word become flesh?"

humanity and the general church,[55] which in turn undid the need to see it as a necessary component of the hierarchical pyramid. The church is still the soul of the *corpus christianum* [Christian body], but this soul no longer dominates.[56] [/32]

(§96) In the second place, he distinguishes not only the revelation of the Creator and of the Redeemer, but also in the former the revelation from out of God's work [*werkstuk*] and that from out of the general doctrine of Scripture.[57] Faith, which answers to the word-revelation communicated to us in Scripture, loses any supernatural signature for it is already present in the state of rectitude, at which time too the word-revelation supplemented inquiry. *This* natural, general word-revelation is, in consequence of the fall, no longer adequate, and it *becomes* supplemented in history itself with the special word-revelation about grace. Believing God's word thereby becomes especially believing the word of mercy.[58] Accordingly, such faith, as viewed by Calvinism, is knowledge of love that calls up love in response, an effect of which is trust.[59]

(§97) Thirdly, we need to attend to the theory of the image of God. Calvin sometimes takes this to mean that by which the human being transcends other animate creatures, at other times he means the original moral purity and rectitude.[60] Hence these two views do not stand over against each other as "lenient" and "strict," but as metaphysical and historical characterizations. The latter is new, and precisely this factor should not be masked by the Aristotelian schema of "lower" and "higher," to which [schema] the current distinction again and again tempt the mystics. Otherwise it becomes unintelligible how the loss this [image]

---

55 J. Bohatec, "De organische idee in de gedachtenwereld van Calvijn" III, *Antirevolutionaire Staatkunde* (July-August 1926): 372.

56 Bohatec, "De organische idee in de gedachtenwereld van Calvijn," 363.

57 *J. Calvini, magni theologi, institutionum christianae religionis libri quattuor, editio postrema* etc., ed. Beza, Lugduni Batavorum, in officio Petri Leffen, 1654, I, II, 1 [Latin quotation in translation: "First, in the fashioning of the universe and in the general teaching of Scripture the Lord shows himself to be the Creator." [John Calvin, *Institutes of the Christian Religion. Library of Christian Classics Vol. 20.;* translated by Ford Lewis Battles (London: SCM, 1961), 40.]

58 M. Schneckenburger, *Vergleichende Darstellung des lutherischen und reformirten Lehrbegriffes,* aus dessen handschriftlichen Nachlasse zusammengestellt und herausgegeben durch E. Güder, I (Stuttgart: Metzler, 1855), 59–60.

59 *Heidelberg Catechism,* Question and Answer 21.

60 A.S.E. Talma, *De anthropologie van Calvijn* (Utrecht: Breyer, 1882), 104. (dissertation)

had earlier can be linked to the complete preservation of the *difference* in essence [compared with other creatures]; – true; this [difference] now reveals itself through the curse on both at a lower level than was formerly the case. Between human beings mutually there is the difference of election to salvation [*zaligheid*]. However the offices belong to the essence that all have in common, although here too the effect is felt as to whether one has or has not received the restorative anointing of Christ. For even though office bearers differ in evincing their subservience and hence in their inclination to follow Christ when exercising them, the call to and the functions of the offices remain unchanged.

(§98) In these offices the human being stands first of all over against God. In the prophetic office the confession of His Name is central.[61] Calvin does not apply a psychological classification to the offices. Sometimes he leaves this [classification] entirely to philosophy, at other times he speaks of *two* capacities: cognition and willing.[62] The three offices [i.e., of prophet, priest, and king] properly belong to the terrain of religion.

(§99) It would be wise, following Calvin in this respect, to advance a bit further and to let the psychologists decide which division best fits the field of inquiry. Calvin remains the illustrious example of "boundary drawer" in a spirit not met with in philosophy either before or after him, this being of course to philosophy's own great detriment. What a pity it was that shortly afterwards Theodore Beza tried to satisfy the need for philosophical training in the Reformed circle in the same way that Philipp Melanchthon had already done for the Lutheran: [/33] by returning to Aristotle. This combination weakened Reformed theology extraordinarily. For first of all one turned to defending, over against the new currents, what on closer inspection showed no principled difference with the spirit of this renewal. And no less so, the weapons one used wounded the hand that wielded them.

(§100) This double danger became even more pressing due to the vagueness of the concept of nature, which became such a determining factor in contemporary developments. Most took the term "*naturalis*" [inborn; regarding nature] to mean "*communis*" [communal; in general] in the historical sense of "in Paradise" and in virtue of the common origin all shared; [but they did so] without taking into account the danger that a small group ran when borrowing terminology, namely of losing the pure

---

61   *Heidelberg Catechism*, Question and Answer 32.
62   J. Calvini, *Calvini, magni theologi, institutionum christianae religionis,* I, 15, 6–8. [J. Calvin, *Institutes of the Christian Religion,* vol. 1, 192–196.]

concept. The consequences soon became apparent: "nature" was again taken and understood in the sense of medium or, put more theologically, as project. In that way "*theologia naturalis*" [natural theology] acquired the meaning of being scientific knowledge about the word-revelation in Paradise and about revelation in the great artistic works of the Creator.[63] Add to that the confusion of knowledge of God and theology, and the individualistic neglect of the difference between the revelation given to the prophets and the communication of their knowledge to the Church, and it becomes clear how damaged Reformed life could not avoid becoming as it emerged from this struggle that was already ignited in the circle of the humanists and in which one, entirely needlessly, took sides.

F. *Renaissance humanism*

(§101) Initially the *Renaissance* – to which I now turn – displayed no inclination at all towards scientific work. The word "renaissance" already says it: one wanted rebirth, but not, as is often assumed, for antiquity but for oneself.[64] Now one must remember that scholasticism had already linked this product of grace [*heilsgoed*] inextricably with the church's administering of baptism,[65] and thus with the "supernatural" terrain. Alighieri Dante had secularized this further and applied it to the "earthly" relations between papacy and empire. Others took it further yet. Italy was awakening and desperately desired freedom. But when the growing longing for the messiah-emperor who was to return this freedom to Italy was not satisfied, the term "rebirth" gained an entirely unchristian sense. Appealing to Augustine's possibly perilous portrayal of Adam in the state of rectitude, some, already quite early, posed as ideal the repristination of this state: "*ut reddamur ad pristinum statum Adae*" ["that we return to the original state of Adam"]. It was now said, evidently in line with the Stoics, that, along with God, nature also works in that direction. In this way the living soul is first idealized to be a living spirit, then the latter is viewed as an ideal to be attained even after the fall in sin and without the

---

63 A. Kuyper, *Encyclopaedie der Heilige Godgeleerdheid*, II, 2nd ed. (Kampen: Kok, 1909), 260–263. "Locus de Deo" I, in A. Kuyper, *Dictaten Dogmatiek* I, 2nd ed. (Kampen: Kok, 1910), 36, means to express, in light of the foregoing, the same thing as the passage in the *Encyclopaedie*. However, the punctuation at the bottom of page 35 and the top of page 36 is not clear.

64 K. Burdach, *Reformation, Renaissance, Humanismus, zwei Abhandlungen über die Grundlage moderner Bildung und Sprachkunst* (Berlin: Paetel, 1918), 13–96.

65 Kuyper, "Locus de Salute" in *Dictaten Dogmatiek* IV, 2nd ed. (Kampen: Kok, 1910), 71 ff.

influence of the life-giving Spirit.[66] Francesco Petrarch speaks of himself in all modesty as *"homo spiritualis"* ["spiritual man"] and Giovanni Pico della Mirandola thinks it is possible to give rebirth to *oneself: "poteris in superiora* [/34] *quae sunt divina ex tui anima sentential regenerari"* ["[It will be in your power to degenerate into the lower forms of life, which are brutish; equally] you shall have the power, according to your soul's judgment, to be reborn into the higher orders, which are divine."][67]

Antiquity is in this connection not a goal but an example, evidently on account of its lack of any Christian ferment. The way to [attain] this regeneration is through competition with nature. Now the Renaissance's concept of nature is certainly not yet that of the modern understanding; for as to its extent, it includes antiquity's and scholasticism's understanding of nature, which agree in this regard. The difference is limited to that of valuation, for the stigma of inferiority is gone. The supernatural is radically removed, like a layer of unnatural veneer. The consequence of course was that the purely unchristian character [of this development] became public, which had remained hidden only by naïvely reading the characteristic thoughts of the Middle Ages into it. In terms of historical understanding this can of course hardly be considered other than pure gain. The only question that remained was how this rediscovery should be evaluated.

(§102) When one once again carefully reviews the traits of the picture sketched above, it comes as no surprise that Aristotle failed to excite unqualified enthusiasm among the majority of Renaissance philosophers, although he was now judged more accurately historically. For though the old metaphysics of essence and appearance was retained, the overrating of the human being could not tolerate its being classified without reserve in the form-matter schema, although this schema was never wholly rejected. In this way, via Augustine – whose valuation of the word revelation was not shared in the least – one returned to the Neoplatonists and the Stoics, both in connection with economic and political theories and also in epistemology.

(§103) But whoever rejects the word revelation retains, in the ambiguous *theologia naturalis* [natural theology], only the knowledge of God as acquired through nature. Now one ought to distinguish sharply this knowledge of *God* from the knowledge of the relations that he created in

---

66 See over against this the thought expressed in 1 Corinthians 15:45.

67 Burdach, *Reformation, Renaissance, Humanismus,* 175–180; translation, cf. http://harpers.org/archive/2008/11/hbc-90003927.

a distinct region. For, however unlimited our striving is in connection with the latter, the attempt to gain knowledge of God in an indirect way, without the help of the *revelatio verbalis communis* [general word revelation], postulates crossing the boundary between God and the cosmos. God has, precisely in the communication of truth about Himself and His connection with the cosmos, taken this course, forbidden to us, but which He took in our direction for our sake.[68]

(§104) Humanism, however, has always rejected this boundary, never doing so more intentionally than in the burgeoning modern period [*nieuwe tijd*]. For antiquity was still acquainted with the dualism of fate and what falls under it. Even Zeus honors it as meekly as the human being [cf. §8]. But fate cannot be known. As soon as this dualism is surmounted by that of God and cosmos, which [two realities], however connected, remain in essence distinct [cf. §9], then *theologia naturalis* [natural theology] becomes an option. As long as one took this to mean the *cognitio Dei* [cognition of God] in Paradise, based on the word revelation, then one could only object to the confusion of knowledge and science. This terminology became more risky when it was applied [/35] by those who, as in Christianity, taught that God is knowable but who rejected the "word revelation in Paradise." Not being satisfied with the knowledge of the [cosmos as] project [*werkstuk*], which other sciences provide us, such persons now strove to attain knowledge of the Creator as gleaned from the project without the help of the word revelation. Mysticism had already confessed to the experienced disappointment in this regard when speaking of "*via negationis*" [the way of denial]. However the Renaissance, though it took the same route, promised to achieve a better result.

(§105) On what ground?

(§106) On the following. The Renaissance secularizes the concept of God, not as antiquity did, but it deifies the individual by raising the latter from its status as a [created] project to a Self-revelation of God. For example, Nicolas Cusanus wrote: "*Creatura igitur est ipsius creatoris sese definientis seu lucis, quae deus est, se ipsam manifestantis ostensio*" ["Therefore, the creature is the manifestation of the Creator defining Himself – or the manifestation of the Light, which is God, manifesting itself"].[69] In this way the problem shifts from theology to metaphysics. After all,

---

68 Cf. Romans 10:6–10.

69 Quote from N. Cusanus, *De non aliud* (1462), cited in E. Cassirer, *Das Erkenntnisproblem in der Philosophie und Wissenschaft der neueren Zeit*, I, 2nd ed. (Berlin: Cassirer, 1911), 24, n. 2.

the cosmic unity [i.e., the individual] cannot be fully known [merely] in terms of a number of circles of consideration [*gezichtsvelden*]. For even if one postulates that this number can be increased indefinitely, then one has thereby not yet adequately accounted for the divine infinity of this deified individual.

(§107) This individual can only be known in terms of his *work*, thereby revealing one's infinitude indirectly. Here the Renaissance differs, in its thirst for activity, from mysticism. For it is not in the allied soul, always no more than half divine, that one's pretended divine infinity reveals itself, but in the *work* of the moreover *complete* human being.

(§108) And now it will also be clear where all this had to lead in epistemology. Here too one felt compelled to look for something created by the human being. It is found in science, and the bud lay already in judgment. Logic for the restless person of the Renaissance is again dialectic, *ars disserendi* [art of dialectics], and truth is sought in the creative connection of moments that don't themselves as yet have truth relevance, but nevertheless are already immanent in the mind.

(§109) This exaggeration of the meaning of science is not native to epistemology. It is foisted onto it by an entirely non-epistemological motive, namely the self-deification of the human being. The person is no longer considered *primus inter pares* [the first among equals], but, as Godlike, is the highest form and the first deed. In that way, though that person doesn't create the material, he/she does create the truth that answers to this material as content: "*mens per se est dei imago et omnia post mentem, non nisi per mentum*" ["thus mind as such is the image of God, and everything dependent on mind only through mind"].[70] For that reason the cosmos is no longer God's project, of which the word revelation speaks to us and the intersections of which, though lacking truth for us, still display a divine arrangement resting on the *logos* [i.e., the logical law-sphere]. No, the truth lies in the human mind, and the order it creates is the only order. What lies outside of this order is a-cosmic being, the Platonic *me on* [non-being], that actually does not belong there. And only what God arranges through the human being may be called "cosmic."

(§110) As with the Neoplatonists, the boundary between subject and object also [/36] becomes one that shifts. Whatever is already arranged

---

70 N. Cusanus, *Idiota* III, 3 fol. 84a; in Cassirer, *Das Erkenntnisproblem*, 37. [Nicholas de Cusa, *Idiota de Mente/The Layman: About Mind*, trans. and intro. by Clyde Lee Miller (New York: Abaris Books, 1979), 51.]

is absorbed by the subject and contributes a share in shaping what remained of the object. The *adaequatio* [equalization, matching] is taken in an active sense. The distinct sense-organs simply pass by what doesn't suit them. In a later stage the image-making capacity collects the result of their operation, and as highest resort the spirit once again intervenes. In and through all these formations the power of the soul reveals itself as designer [*vormend*].

(§111) This is why the interest is also shifted from the traditional object to the method of its fashioning [*vorming*]. The object, the thing, is objection, to be overcome, though as a-logical hindrance it is never completely overcome. The *thing* is changed into resistance. The cosmos of the order of truth can only be established in the welter of sense-perceptions. On the other hand our work is never completed, being creative in nature. The sequence of the fields [of inquiry], which can be deduced from the organization of the methods, here becomes the arrangement of the methods of objectification. In the lead there is the point of the mind, through memory and motion the line is fashioned, then, with the help of this line, [the] number [sequence] is formed. What is once fashioned becomes [in turn] a factor of the form; constantly enriched in this way, it [the fashioning subject] progressively fashions the remaining material.

(§112) In this system, in addition to the exaggeration of science and method, the one-sided interest in natural science speaks for itself. The material to be fashioned is the segue to the respective content, namely matter. Now, when accepting this task, number already resides with the subject, not because – as in Plato – there is no place for it with the object, itself split in essence and appearance, but because it is said to offer less resistance when fashioning it. In this way natural science becomes mathematical. Hence the reason for this is not because the world of numbers is the first sphere known to us that follows upon the *logos* [i.e., logical law-sphere] in the cosmic order, so that the other spheres, except the *logos*, rest on it and exhibit a progressively heavier encumbrance in the analogy; rather, the reason is that space offers the occasion to construct in thought a systematic unity of the relations in which the cosmos is now taken to exist.[71] For it [space] belongs to the form, which, in connection with the new content, is itself said to lack content. In that way formal truth [*inhoudslooze waarheid*] is all there is; the rest must first be scientifically and pre-scientifically organized, but it displays no affinity at all for such treatment.

---

71   Cassirer, *Das Erkenntnisproblem*, 29.

G. *Post-Renaissance humanism and science*

(§113) I have intentionally given a rather broad account of the late-Renaissance♦ theory of knowledge, for two reasons. In the first place, newly discovered truth and errors of old are very closely intertwined here, and the separation of both is a life-necessity for everyone who wishes to analyze knowledge. But also [secondly] a longer discussion of this topic is able to shorten the sequel considerably.

(§114) In this milieu the first thing that confronts us is a link between the old error concerning the relation between God and the human being and a new discovery of the greatest importance, in consequence of which [/37] the old metaphysics and the special sciences now part ways. [The discovery is that] the aim of a special science is to determine the relations between moments [of the content of a field of inquiry], and that such a determination progresses within a circle of consideration [*gezichtsveld*]. In light of the results achieved, this process can be called *concept formation*.

(§115) But here too error has mutilated the new beyond recognition. First of all, the theory of the object immanent to the mind confuses judgment with concept, and thus it appears, erroneously, as if concept formation and judgment formation coalesce. All truth here is then judgment truth. Now these [judgment truths] indeed arise when pronouncing judgment, for the latter is an activity aimed at the value of an earlier intuitive or conceptually grasped truth possession. Thus when pronouncing a judgment of relation, a real concept is already possessed by the mind. However, truth itself is not identical to judgment truth. Truth first appears when assimilating knowledge [*kennisverwerking*], [whereas] in knowledge acquisition [*kennisverwerving*] it is the desired good. For knowledge is truth in possession; it is not [the result of] distinguishing, which indeed begins with sense-perception and – this holds of comparison too – is much broader than knowledge.

Identifying that which is non-logical and truths about the same is clearly out of line. But that is no reason to consider truth to be of our own making, the way a concept in a certain sense may be said to be. So too, the non-logical is not a-cosmic; for there are other laws of God than such as hold for truth acquisition, and all these law-spheres lie in the cosmos created by Him. Also, although matter is the object when it comes to sense-perception, that is no reason to take it to be the limit of the ideal

---

♦[Reading "laat-Renaissance" for "na-Renaissance"; cf. also §120; A.T.]

of objectification. Matter is present, along with perception, in the sphere of knowledge only as inducement and as knowable referent [*gekende*].

So too, the whole personality is active in both knowing and perceiving, which is not to say that these activities lie in each other's extension. In perceiving the soul is focused by means of the sense-organs on matter within or outside of the body, but when knowing, the soul points at truth. That is why in science perception merely plays the role of the means of double-checking the accuracy of a calculation concerning the coincidence of a point [i.e., position] and the motion of a material object.[72] And finally, in concept formation the form is indeed without content. When there is reference to space in doing physics, this is owing not to the form but to the circle of consideration [of physics]; physical space is an analogy of pure space.

(§116) So the arguments against modern humanism form a long concatenation. But all relate to the central error, namely, God in us controls the world through us according to the nature of our essence. In continually renewed protest this is protested against, also by those who lack the time and the inclination to be active in the theory of knowledge. For if God has indeed called us to rule over the work of his hands, then our qualification is determined not only by our essence as such but also by the law of the connection between us and these works. [/38]

(§117) But, as was said, one ought to distinguish the good and the bad [*kwade*] elements. Those who fail to do so return, as had Beza and Melanchthon, to Aristotle, and mistake the value of the new concept of science, which rejects both Aristotelian teleology and the dualism of Plato that Aristotle was the first to reduce to a higher unity. For matter is not the "appearance" of an essence or thing, but exclusively the correlate of the perceiver. That is why natural science [i.e., physics] does not concern itself with matter but with energy and the structure of material things. That is also why, with Galileo, the natural sciences came into conflict with the Greek preference for that which is immutable and immovable, a preference that still holds sway in Johannes Kepler.[73] Whoever distinguishes truth about energy from truth about motion must choose for science in this conflict and against the aesthetic approach. But then one

---

72 For more detailed discussion, cf. D.H.Th. Vollenhoven, "Kentheorie en natuurwetenschap," section III, *Orgaan der Christelijke Vereeninging van Natuur- en Geneeskundigen in Nederland*, (no. 4, 1926): 147–197. [Vollenhoven has "no. 3" and no page-reference; he anticipated its appearing in the third issue of 1926; A.T.]

73 E. Goldbeck, "Der Untergang des kosmischen Weltbildes der Antike," *Die Antike, Zeitschrift für Kunst und Kultur des klassischen Altertums* I (1925): 61–79.

also needs to clearly distinguish between perception and knowledge and all of their correlates, hence not only between matter and the material of concepts but also between world picture and natural science.[74] Doing so helps one make sense of the fact that we perceive matter moving only when we don't share its motion, and, at the same time, fail to notice the motion we do share, even though the experiment agrees with the calculation of the coincidence of matter and point [i.e., position].

H. *Modern rationalism*

(§118) Humanism did not clearly distinguish perception and knowledge. As a result the conflict at this time between rationalism and empiricism – "phenomenalism" would be the better term – is really just about [the apportioning of] more or less [of either component]. For that reason I can, with one exception [cf. §162], ignore empiricism – a critique of its main intention would lead to a monotonous repetition and to attend to details would continually deflect further away from what is of logical and epistemological importance.

(§119) With rationalism the situation is different. Rationalism combines proto-attempts to "purify" knowledge of any admixture with perception with a most egregious exaggeration of the autonomous subject, which, when absorbing the logical form into itself, becomes *ratio*. The attempt to purge knowledge of perception was doomed to fail, time and again, not so much because of its preference for geometry – which is not general – but especially because, here too, thought and perception continue to be seen in a teleological connection. But because the influence of perception was indeed reduced to a minimum, I will put this main objection, which holds across the board, to the side and, with an eye to avoiding unnecessary detours, focus on a critique of what each thinker considers to be the crux of the matter.

1. *Prominent seventeenth century figures*

(§120) We have seen how the theory of knowledge of the Renaissance came to exaggerate the meaning of science as enterprise, all the while imposing upon this enterprise the demands of the method of doing physics. Doing so was both unjustified as well as ill-conceived, for the boundaries of the [/39] circle of consideration of mechanics were not yet clearly determined; for example, one could praise Galileo for excluding some

---

74 Hence my objection to identifying image and knowledge of physics, as for example in W.J. A. Schouten, "Het wereldbeeld van den Bijbel," *Orgaan der Christelijke Ver-eeniging van Natuur- en Geneeskundigen in Nederland* (no. 2, 1926): 68 ff.

sense-qualities when determining his field of inquiry, and just as easily fault him for not being more radical in this regard. For, in this connection, the distinction between primary and secondary qualities, which he adopted from Democritus, has no relevance – whatever its value might be elsewhere – for determining the extent of physics' circle of consideration; *neither* of these qualities pertain here.[75] That said, this distinction did provide the basis for the this-is-what-it-looks-like preference that classical mechanics undoubtedly had. However, this preference is a psychological one and ought not dominate the science of energy a moment longer now that its character is fathomed. As long as this was not the case, one couldn't help but confuse matter, unjustly robbed of some of its qualities, with energy; confusing the maimed object of perception with a field of scientific inquiry, the determination of which is totally different.

Thus René Descartes couldn't help but conclude that the method of physics was most appropriate for the study of bodies, i.e., for all that is perceptible.[76] Accordingly, not only was this detrimental to biology, but also psychology again paid the price. For "to know of" ["*weet van*"] became the organ of inner perception, and carried the pretension of having knowledge value – those who perceived what was going on within soon presumes the role of psychologist. And of course the knowing subject again [unjustly] became a part of the soul.

One may respect Descartes' attempt to distinguish judgment and willing from conceptual understanding;[77] after all, that concept and rep-

---

75 Th.L. Haering, *Philosophie der Naturwissenschaft, Versuch eines einheitlichen Ver-ständnisses der Methoden und Ergebnisse der (anorganischen) Naturwissenschaft. Zu-gleich eine Rehabilitierung des vorwissenschaftlichen Weltbildes* (München: Rösl & Cie, 1923), 328, 333.

76 A.G.A. Balz, *Dualism in Cartesian Psychology and Epistemology* (New York: Columbia University Press, 1925), especially 130–153.

77 Renati Des-Cartes, *Meditationes de prima philosophia* etc., secunda editio septimis objectionibus antehac non visis aucta, Amstelodami apud Ludovicum Elzevirium, 1642, 27/30; especially [Meditation] III [/74] [A long Latin quotation, then the closing remark:] "See also *Objectio V and VI ad meditationem tertiam*, 203 ff., *Responsio*, 205 ff., and *Objectio VI*, 206 ff. with *Responsio*."
[The quotation is from the third Meditation: "Of God: that He exists": "I shall now close my eyes, I shall stop my ears, I shall call away all my senses, I shall efface even from my thoughts all the images of corporeal things, or at least (for that is hardly possible) I shall esteem them as vain and false; and thus holding converse only with myself and considering my own nature, I shall try little by little to reach a better knowledge of and a more familiar acquaintanceship with myself. I am a thing that thinks, that is to say, that doubts, affirms, denies, that knows a few things, that is ignorant of many [that loves, that hates], that wills, that desires, that also imagines and perceives. . . ." "And in order that I may have an opportunity of inquiring into

resentation remain together in this way is not the worst as such. But that cannot be said about the confusion of theory of knowledge and psychology. On the one hand psychology is enormously exaggerated, but on the other hand it loses a part of its terrain. For the psychologist is concerned equally with the "knowing of" as with acts that Descartes very characteristically calls *cogitationes* [thoughts], evidently in the sense of immediately perceived cognition. The theory of knowledge suffers even greater damage. For whoever maintains that perception affords knowledge can never avoid skepticism.

Even the veracity of God, called upon here to help, cannot prevent the identification of two terrains, even less does that keep perception from becoming vaguer – *ceteris paribus* [other things being equal] – as the distance between the perceiver and the perceived increases. Certainly, God's power holds body and soul together. But it does more: it also maintains the connection between the moments in one and the same law-sphere. Yet both activities – preserving a cosmic unity [i.e., an individual] that is intersected by different law-spheres, and maintaining the moments within a law-sphere according to its nature – should certainly be kept distinct.

(§121) For Baruch Spinoza both activities refer back to a higher unity. He too proceeds from the subject-object dualism, but he attributes to [/40] the object also what he knows about himself, namely the whole object of perception, inner and outer together. That object is space, which, given this perspective on representations, is completely justified. Focusing oneself on this object, thought of as primal substance, takes place with such complete surrender as is only fitting over against God. Intuitive knowledge, which is knowledge of the third or the highest kind, is limited to geometry. The number of the attributes of space is infinite, only two of which fall under the second kind of knowledge, namely that of general concepts, these being cognition and extension, which unlike Descartes,

---

this in an orderly way . . . it is requisite that I should here divide my thoughts into certain kinds. . . . Of my thoughts some are, so to speak, images of the things, and of these alone is the title 'idea' properly applied; examples are my thought of a man or of a chimera, of heaven, of an angel, or [even] of God. But other thoughts possess other forms as well. For example in willing, fearing, approving, denying, though I always perceive something as the subject of the action of my mind, yet by this action I always add something else to the idea which I have of that thing; and of the thoughts of this kind some are called volitions or affections, and others judgments." *The Philosophical Works of Descartes*, translated by E.S. Haldane and G.R.T. Ross, Vol. I. (Cambridge: At the University Press, 1972), 157 and 159; the square brackets are those of Haldane and Ross; A.T.]

Spinoza sharply distinguishes from space. The first or the lowest kind of knowledge has the passive and confused traits of sensation and memory. At this level the two lines, initially kept so carefully apart, again merge.[78]

Nicolas Malebranche identifies God not with the object but with *cogitata* [thoughts]. God is the situs of spirits, the way extension is the place of bodies. "We see all things in God" is merely the pious formulation of the statement that the subject perceives the outer world of things via the medium of *cogitationes* [thoughts]. The latter limit the idea of God in the same way that bodies limit extension.[79]

(§122) This resulted in all of philosophy bowing to a science that was simply unable to clearly determine the boundaries of its field of inquiry. And because no one noticed a difference between representation and thought, other than a quantitative one, criticism was doomed to fail from the start. Blaise Pascal, it is true, did oppose scientialism in the name of Christianity, but his protest sounds more passionate than persuasive. He begins his analysis of the experiment by accepting what he will later reject as being insufficient. As in Augustine, a little pagan temple is erected within the church of the system; this attests more to piety towards what is ancient than to historical awareness and a concept of style. However much the critical *Lettres provinciales* may elicit admiration, the positive *Penseés* are weak; that its logic was not acknowledged even by the monks of Port Royal evinces the telling independence of his followers. For it is not our understanding that needs to be crucified for the sake of a religion said to possess the certainty of the impossible,[80] but only what is carnal in the understanding; an understanding that forgets, also in this description of religion, that what is not possible for human beings need not on that account be impossible in an absolute sense. Dialectical religion is in the deepest sense irreligious, for it again measures♦ God by the human measure. So just as Pascal, with good reason, compares Rome to Peter, who slept while Jesus struggled in Gethsemane,[81] this simile tempts me spontaneously to remind those who, like Pascal, wrongly fancy themselves followers

---

78   B. Spinoza, *Ethica* II, Propositio XL.

79   A. Buchenau, "Über den Begriff des Unendlichen und der intelligiblen Anschauung bei Malebranche und die Beziehung der letzteren zum Kantischen Raumbegriff," *Kant-Studien* 14:4 (1909): 440–467.

80   L. Schestow, "Die Nacht zu Gethsemané (Pascals philosophie)"; vom Verfasser durchgesehene Uebersetzung aus dem Russischen von Hans Ruoff, in *Ariadne, Jahrbuch der Nietzsche-Gesellschaft* (1925), 36–109, especially 52.

81   Schestow, "Die Nacht zu Gethsemané," 36.

of Paul, of Eutychus – who, according to Luke [Acts 20:9], nearly lost his life upon sinking into a deep sleep during the teaching of the great apostle to the heathen. [/41]

2. G.W. Leibniz

(§123) It is no wonder that Pascal's critique could no more bring the theory of knowledge to repentance than that the intuitionism of Émile Boutroux and Henri Bergson would later be able to undo Neo-Kantianism. For Leibniz continues, at least in the main, to build unperturbed on the old foundations. Although geometry did have to offer priority to arithmetic,[82] which narrows somewhat the meaning of representation, his rationalism remains mathematical, and the representation is still the precursor [*praeformatie*] of the concept. The difference in quantum of motion, measured at a particular time and place according to the method of the differential calculus, is transformed, by virtue of his egregious arithmetism [*arithmetisme*], from a conceptual magnitude of physics into a metaphysical non-extension, though this is still thought of as an atom in a definite position. The kernel of this atom is called "soul" – as the judgment of the theory about the perception of animate fellow creatures would have it – while the body is the visible outline or appearance from which two forms can be abstracted: space and time. The point of departure here is not the sphere with its laws, but the individual living substance. In order to warrant its self-sufficiency it is assumed that the Creator has placed a view of the world within the soul, such that this monad requires no windows. Awareness and concept are to each other as the states of sleeping and wakefulness. They differ only in degree of clarity. That is why all knowledge is rooted in the spatial distinction in the organization of our environment; for the *principium identitatis indiscernibilium* [principle of the identity of indiscernibles] changes [in use] from being a postulate of physical measuring to a logico-epistemological principle. Truth, too, is immanent to the subject; it being the agreement of judgment and knowledge. Even though this limits science to matter in motion and everything takes place according to a mechanical order, this does not exclude goal-directedness. As a brilliant engineer God maintains the order by means of which everything takes place both mechanistically and with teleological intent. The difference between causal science and universal teleology is not one of field [of inquiry] but of *direction* and

82   H. Schmalenbach, *Leibniz* (München: Drei Maskenverlag, 1921), 31 ff.

◆[Reading "meet" for "meer" (more); A.T.]

way of viewing. For Leibniz to call these the "kingdom of nature" and the "kingdom of grace" [respectively] is an abuse of history; up to that point these terms had a totally different meaning.

(§124) In Leibniz the distinction of necessary truths and contingent truths is also important. A truth is necessary whose content is "timeless," such as for example the truths of the theory of space. It is impossible to ever assert meaningfully the denial of such a truth. Impossibility finds its negative expression in the *principium contradictionis* [principle of contradiction], its positive expression in [the principle of] identity. According to Leibniz, one does not come across this impossibility in contingent truths, i.e., in judgments made on the basis of knowledge about something that is intersected♦ by the sphere of time. Hence "possibility" is the modality of all non-geometrical truths; judgments which, once made, one could imagine to have been otherwise. However, when doing so one misses reality, which is seen in relation to [/42] possibility as the fulfillment of a specific possibility.[83]

(§125) Now one should clearly distinguish in Leibniz between space and time on the one hand and method on the other. Space and time, as in all vitalism, are said to be abstracted from matter. They are in that sense not absolute: one proceeds from the object of perception as correlate of thought, via an abstraction that is immanent to mind, to what one hopes is a kind of general representation of space and time. Being abstracted, space and time are not absolute; the theories of space and of time owe their origin, unlike arithmetic, to mathematical physics.

(§126) Just as mechanism threatened the independence of biology and psychology, vitalism is a threat to physics and even more so to the theory of space and time. If it was only a matter of protecting each science's field of inquiry then one could ascribe this conflict to the short-sightedness

---

83 D. Baumgardt, *Das Möglichkeitsproblem der Kritik der einen Vernunft, der modernen Phänomenologie und der Gegenstandstheorie* (Berlin: Reuther & Reichard, 1921), 9, 10.

♦[Reading "intersected" for "not intersected." Examples of "timeless truths," besides those of geometry, are also those of arithmetic and of logic itself. Contingent truths entail a reference to time or anything of higher modality based on time, such as motion, physical interaction, organic life, etc. Thus the non-geometrical truths, once formulated, which "one could imagine to have been otherwise," are those of higher modality, not the lower ones of arithmetic or logic; A.T.]

of two groups of specialists, and fault each group for pursuing a[n illicit] policy of expansion. But this is an incorrect assessment and should be rejected. The conflict between specialists can always be resolved by calling to mind the limitation of the methods in use. Differences in method are correlated to differences between the [respective] circles of consideration. The error of both mechanism and vitalism is, however, that one attempts to derive a classification for the sciences from what, according to the Scripture, is a cosmological-historical difference [of dead and living]. But however many law-spheres history may intersect, it does not determine the [distinct] *character* of any one of these. This holds both for the realistic-Aristotelian view of this classification, which equates the living with what is higher and the dead with what is lower, and for the methodological-Leibnizian view, which takes the teleological method to be correlated to what lives and the causal method to what is dead – the latter erroneously equated with what is non-animate. Matter is not dead material, but the correlate [or the object] of perception, also as regards plants, animals, and human beings. Physics does not concern itself with matter but with the circle of consideration of energy, as far as it extends. So too biology ought to consider it beneath its dignity to justify its independence – though the latter be readily admitted – by calling on something other than its own method; or, at a deeper level: appealing to the independence of its own circle of consideration. But also this circle of consideration will turn out to intersect♦ cosmic essences [e.g., individuals], whose unity needs to be maintained not by it [i.e., biology] but by cosmology.

(§127) Leibniz, as we saw, seeks a solution in a different way. He places the synthetic method over against the abstracting method of analysis, which besides seeking Aristotelian fundamental concepts also looks for fundamental judgments,[84] finding these in the science of numbers [*arithmetiek*]. But both are cosmological. The synthetic is the complicating [*compliceerende*] [method], which, proceeding from number, is bound up with arithmetical proof. By investigating the "coherence of

---

84 B. Jansen, *Leibniz erkenntnistheoretischer Realist. Grundlinien seiner Erkenntnislehre* (Berlin: Simion 1920), 8–15.

♦ [Literally: "apply a cross-section through." The intersection is that of a general determination of being that *characterizes,* essentially, an individual thing. Most things (except numbers) have, as characterized, many such "cross-section" intersects; as suggested by J.H. Kok, A.T.]

truth" in this [complicating] direction, method serves to discover the levels of connection that secure or support [*stavingssamenhang*]; understanding becomes [the process of] securing the higher circle of consideration on the basis of the lower one(s). Naturally that cannot succeed. Leibniz does not see the difference among circles [/43] of consideration, and also takes securing a composite concept by a more elementary [concept] in a specific field – that of arithmetic – as the initial realization of his ideal. When he can go no further he attributes this to human finitude; for God, however, also contingent truths are well-founded.

(§128) That sounds very reverent, yet it is anything but that. For God doesn't build one concept upon another – unless this be in His Word-revelation, in which He places Himself under the law for the sake of His covenant. He created cosmic unities in such a way that they are intersected by different law-spheres. Law-spheres are arranged in such a way that everything rests on the logical [law-sphere]. This also enables humanity to fulfill its academic-scientific calling, namely to trace the analogical [moments] in the different circles. Complex concepts can be built from simpler ones, but never without taking into account the boundaries within which this takes place, because otherwise one immediately stumbles on an antinomy.

(§129) Arithmetical rationalism too neglected that. The superficiality of Christian Wolff even made him forget the [boundary] limitation – which he saw at most as being merely temporary – and with it the distinction of necessary and contingent truths. This led to various derivations: possibility could be derived from necessity, the principle of sufficient reason (in Leibniz's meaning) from that of identity and contradiction, [and] the biotic and the physical from the mathematical – for in Wolff the difference between arithmetic and geometry also recedes into the background.

3. *I. Kant*
(§130) The foregoing enables us to address Immanuel Kant. Because I am of the opinion that his mistake lies in *the way the problem* to which the *Critique of Pure Reason* provides the answer *is posed*, the method [of our discussion] – we'll need to concentrate on essentials here – is prescribed of itself: the query "Is synthesis a priori possible?" needs to be investigated, and the suspicion that his pre-critical works provide us with most of what we are looking for is indeed confirmed.

(§131) Kant takes the subject to be substantive. He shares this standpoint with all his predecessors, both rationalists and empiricists, hence also with Leibniz, with whom however he differs in the theory about monads not having windows. That is why the notion of the representation of the world as pre-formed in the subject, which only needs to be clarified through analysis, loses its value for him.

Kant did not immediately state this as clearly as he did later. Thus his first work, *Gedanken von der wahren Schätzung der lebendigen Kräfte* (1746), offers no more than a step back behind Wolff with respect to the distinction of geometrical and physical truths as necessary and contingent [respectively].[85] In his dissertation, thus nine years later, he no longer adheres to this [distinction], evidently upon realizing that the opposition of necessary and contingent does not determine the boundary between geometry and physics.[86]

In his *Versuch den Begriff der negativen Grössen in die Weltweisheit einzufüren* (1763) [/44] we see what he is after. In that work the opposition between necessary and contingent makes way for the more traditional one of logical *form* and real *content*.[87] Kant would have come further if he had disengaged this logical form from both judgment and the subject. But that did not happen. On the contrary, he takes the logical form to be analytical in the Leibnizian sense. That obliges him, when formulating his desire to increase knowledge, to speak of synthesis. Doing so is tenuous as long as one does not specify how and between what the synthesis is to be realized, especially in light of the promiscuous use of judgment and thought. For synthesis can occur both when judging and in concepts, except that in the latter truth-moments enter into a synthesis, while in the former simple judgments come together. Thus there is synthesis both when assimilating knowledge [in judgments] and when acquiring it [in concepts].

(§132) The forms of sensibility were soon added to the logical form. That Kant placed the apriority of space prior to its boundaries is an improvement compared to Leibniz. [In general,] a modality is a priori with

---

85   I. Kant, *op. cit.*, especially III, §129. [Cf. *Kant Werke*, herausgegeben von Wilhelm Weischedel (Darmstadt: Wissenschaftliche Buchgesellschaft, 1975), Band 1: *Vorkritische Schriften bis 1768*; "Gedanke von der wahren Schätzung der lebendigen Kräfte," chapter III, §129, 183–185.]

86   I. Kant, "Principiorum primorum cognitionis metaphysicae nova dilucidatio etc.," in E. Cassirer, *Immanuel Kants Werke* I (Berlin: Cassirer, 1912–1922). [*Kant Werke*, ed. by Wilhelm Weischedel, 1975, Band 1: *Vorkritische Schriften bis 1768*, 401–509.]

87   Kant, *op. cit.*, III, in Cassirer, *Immanuel Kants Werke* III, 227 ff. [*Kant Werke*, ed. by Wilhelm Weischedel, 1975, Band 2: *Vorkritische Schriften bis 1768*, "Versuch den Begriff der negativen Grössen in die Weltweisheit einzufüren," 777–819.]

respect to all boundaries introduced on its terrain. But one must not be misled by just the sound of a word. For soon *a priori* is taken to be "belonging to the subject," and then *synthesis a priori* means "synthesis realized on the part of the subject." Thus Kant no longer considers mathematics to be analytic but synthetic; although he retains the notion of securing [*staving*] the circles of consideration that lie higher in the order as well as the connection of synthesis in general with the [method of] complication and concept formation.

(§133) But one must pay particular attention to the connection of the correlation "a priori – a posteriori" with that of "subject and object."

(§134) As such, the former correlation has nothing to do with the latter. In this context "a priori" – if I now limit myself to the discussion of just one of the correlates – has no less than four meanings, namely a psychological, a truth-theoretical, an order-theoretical, and a concept-theoretical one. In light of the drabness of the term, this is no surprise. One needs to clearly distinguish this fourfold use if one is to make headway with Kant. So first a brief word about each of these four.

(§135) The psychological meaning of "a priori" is not much more than: present earlier in the psychical world of the individual. Although "a priori" does not actually have this meaning in Kant, his defenders ought to realize that his a priori-concept is not unambiguous simply because it is not tainted by individualistic psychologism. To make this claim requires that one needs first to review the whole series of meanings. For the sake of clarity I simply offer examples of the remaining three, intentionally chosen so as to ease drawing the conclusion regarding Kant when coming to that.

(§136) For example, space is a priori with respect to its boundaries in a truth-theoretical sense. [/45]

(§137) Order-theoretical apriority is somewhat more difficult to grasp. To that end we need the help of methodological notions. Method is *journey*; in the theory of knowledge it is the journey toward the adequate concept, which, as regards its content, is identical with the particular truth one wants to grasp. Now such a truth lies in one of the many circles of consideration, which God has placed in a determinate *order*. That is why the method appropriate to a higher [more complex] circle of consideration can make use of analogies [of less complex circles of consideration] that the Creator has Himself laid there. Now, in reference to this order, the mathematical circles of consideration are a priori with respect to that of energy [because they are lower, or less complex]. This means that I can go a long way in physics with mathematical methods, encumbered [with physical states of affairs]; but methods gleaned from physics are of no use in mathematics.

(§138) Finally, "a priori" has a concept-theoretical meaning. While the theory of knowledge could only offer aid in determining the apriority of order, in the theory of concept formation it is in its own element. For, in connection with concept formation, one finds on the one hand the system of relation-with-its-relata, on the other hand a specific truth. The system is logical in nature and, retaining that character, first plays the role of *form* over against truth as content in the process of concept formation. As soon as this form is encumbered [with content], what encumbers can be called "a priori" with respect to whatever is added to it later.

(§139) Let us now return to Kant with these distinctions in mind..

(§140) The a priori that he seems to have noticed in 1762 in the relationship of space and spatial boundaries must now be characterized as truth-theoretical; the precedence of space to physics as order-theoretical.

(§141) We had found earlier that Kant, like Leibniz, confuses concept-theoretical synthesis with the complicating [direction in] concept formation. Placing the form in the subject, which actively connects form and content, makes for Kant's giving the form an active cachet, as the Neoplatonists had done. Form becomes forming [*vorming*], just as order turns into arranging [*ordening*]. So now, rather than engaging the task of handling the logical system as concept-theoretical form also when forming complicating concepts, the subject is called to something much higher, namely being permitted to secure the higher circles of consideration. The emphasis no longer lies, as in Leibniz, in the sphere of judgments but in that of concepts; hence the reference to the expansion of knowledge, of synthesis between form and content. But form is fashioning by the mind, which is why such a synthesis is a priori.

(§142) So we find that, also here, "form-content" is equated with "subject-object." Sense-awareness, however, is the material. In connection with this duality, *phusis* (nature) is always positioned on the side of the object, and number, space, and time on the side of the subject. Hence mathematics is also synthetic a priori, while physics and metaphysics are not. The mind, [/46] which arranges everything, acts as [if it is] free from the process of science, which is merely concerned with ordering the phenomenal world. Contrary to David Hume *cum suis* [and those with him],

Kant is not interested in the psychical connection of representations in the mind, but rather in the mind's *work*, namely the methodical induction of phenomena. This takes place according to the original laws of the mind, which, being before all else activity, can apparently only come into its own in an anthropocentric metaphysics, now viewed as *ethics*. So we find that already in 1768 the mutual relation of *Sollen* [ought] and *Sein* [being] is determined in a form that is typical for Kant and all his followers. The moral life is not a terrain, however high it may lie in the cosmic order, that can be investigated scientifically like other regions. The humanistic standpoint indeed leads necessarily to this conclusion: the subject that secures order is not itself subject to its laws, and one simply does not acknowledge anything higher than human arranging.

(§143) Kant had not advanced that far yet in 1768 in his answer to the [problem of the] relation between concept and perception. Space and time, because(!) they are not abstracted, still belong to the ideas of the pure understanding.[88] They appear as forms of sensibility for the first time in the inaugural address, i.e., in 1770. What led Kant to take this step? – nothing other than the form-material schema of Aristotelian metaphysics. Knowing is judging, and judgment par excellence belongs to the scientific habitat in which concepts are connected. There need to be concepts – as was correctly concluded initially – prior to the(se) judgments. But the concept is the form with respect to what is lower. Hence it does not require a content but some material, which, like the concept, is psychologically immanent as well. This material is indeed not the last [possibility] – for Kant rejects the view that monads lack windows – but it is that for the scientist and the epistemologist. For sensibility [*aanschouwing*] fills as material the higher form; the latter in turn raises the truth-less material to [the level of] knowledge.

Now this material is given to *us*, *human beings*, in sense perception, which itself assumes forms, not forms of thought but pure forms of sensibility, *intuitus puri* [pure intuition],[89] namely space and time. In this way *our* science is limited to knowledge of phenomena, though there is the possibility of the existence of other groups of creatures whose perceptions

---

88 I. Kant, "Von dem ersten Grunde des Unterschiedes der Gegenden im Raume," in Cassirer, *Immanuel Kants Werke* II, especially 399–400. [Edition Weischedel, 1975, Band 2: *Vorkritische Schriften bis 1768*, 991–1000.]

89 I. Kant, "De mundi sensibilis atque intelligibilis forma et principiis," in Cassirer, *Kants Werke* II, 400–436, especially 408 ff. [Edition Weischedel, 1975, Band 5: *Schriften zur Metaphysik und Logik*, "De mundi sensibilis…" / "Von der Vorm der Sinnen- und Verstandeswelt und ihren Gründen," 7–107.]

– something knowledge can never be without – are arranged differently. In this way Kant thinks he can maintain over against *rationalism* the distinction of logic and mathematics, and over against *empiricism* the subjective apriority of mathematical judgments, which he thinks are presupposed in physics. The *Kritik der reinen Vernunft* deduces the categories, as forms of knowledge, from the essence of the latter. Since knowledge is entirely immanent to the subject, the deduction too needs to proceed from the double synthesis as realized by this subject. First of all Kant finds the "pure" forms of judgment through a desperate identification (that I cannot go into here) of knowing-theoretical, truth-theoretical, judgment-theoretical, and concept-theoretical [/47] motives. A second deduction is necessary in light of the material. And because one must keep open the possibility of a material that is arranged differently, the schema serves to bind the forms of judgment to those [forms] that are specific to the human material.

(§144) Accordingly, one finds firmed up in the first *Critique* what was still unstable in works prior to it. It elaborates a system whose idealistic character clearly emerges already in the way the problem is posed. I hope to have adequately shown that the problem was wrongly posed. There are no scientific synthetic judgments a priori in Kant's sense. Every judgment of science is synthetic, its content is scientific knowledge, and the latter is never a priori: not in the sense of innate concepts, nor in the sense of innate form. The only form used in scientific knowledge acquisition is logical in nature, and all content is gained from the analogy of the logical [law-sphere found] in the plethora of differing states of affairs. That is why all concepts, including mathematical ones, are synthetic but never a priori.

Now, as for the applicability of mathematics to *phusis*♦ [nature]: this should first of all not be exaggerated, for although energy quanta can be calculated, they cannot be constructed mathematically. Also the possibility of calculation rests on an a priori of arrangement [*orde*] that is not applied by means of the logical form, let alone by knowledge, but quite simply come upon. Now a logic may be called transcendental only to the extent that it is in a position to unpack the insight *that* knowledge a priori can be applied and *how* this [can be realized]. That not being the case, transcendental logic must be rejected as pretentious. The same is naturally true – realize: the conflict truly is not about a word but about the autonomy of reason! – for every theory of knowledge that secures the

---

♦[Reading "physis" for "psysis" (*sic*); A.T.]

apriority either of the logical form or of one circle of consideration vis-à-vis another in the subject, or deeper yet, in the Self.

4. *Absolute idealism: J.G. Fichte, F.W.J. Schelling, G.W.F. Hegel*
(§145) Positing methodic thought is insufficient warrant for the commission that human beings secure order. Methodological thinking needs to be founded too. What is it then rooted in?

(§146) That is the question Fichte and Hegel pose. Two moments in the background of their response ought to be distinguished. The first is the aversion of the form-material schema, which by and large makes way for the form-content schema. Perception is a distinct form of being conscious of something. Now had the conclusion been drawn of there being a distinct content correlate to this, something would indeed have been gained. While the material here is indeed no longer the "not yet," it is still the *me on* [non-being]. Perception is not to be assimilated but conquered; and philosophy is only concerned with the *sciences*, hence with the enterprise of humankind to the extent that it has already succeeded in conquering this material.[90] Thinking is transformed from "reshaping-perceptual-material" into "shaping- content," [/48] [i.e.] the category of the manner of reshaping turns into the manner of shaping [as such], the character of which depends on the stadium reached in the shaping process.

[As to the second moment,] although it is clear that thought is not rooted in perception, the "form-content" schema still needs buttressing. All knowledge presupposes one or more metaphysical points of support. In the case at hand, where the human being replaces God, it can only find rest on one side, namely in the free Self.[91] That is Fichte's solution, who, without noticing it however, thereby hits upon an antinomy, namely that the Self that creates knowledge must itself be unknowable, while the theory nevertheless sheds light on this.[92] This problem, which for the humanist is insoluble, still torments his [Fichte's] followers – as one of the most recent publications of Heinrich Rickert attests.[93]

---

90   E. von Aster, *Neukantianismus und Hegelianismus, Eine philosophiegeschichtliche Parallele, in Münchener philosophische Abhandlungen Theodor Lipps zu seinem sechzigsten Geburtstag gewidmet von früheren Schülern* (Leipzig: Barth, 1911), 1–25, especially 10.

91   R. Kroner, *Von Kant bis Hegel*, I (Tübingen: Mohr [Paul Siebeck], 1921), 381–392.

92   R.J. Kortmulder, "Van Kant tot Hegel," *Tijdschrift voor Wijsbegeerte* 20:2 (1926): 141–155, especially 147.

93   H. Rickert, "Von Anfang der Philosophie," *Logos* 14:2/3 (1925): 121–162.

(§147) Schelling took a somewhat different tack. He too wants to creatively secure the form-content schema, but does so by proceeding from the side of the content. Behind this content lies an absolute and creative origin, nature, which in the historical process of cosmogony also brings forth this schema. Spirit [*geest*], i.e., the subject, becomes the attained destination.[94] But here too an antinomy reveals itself: that which is creative, though prior to knowledge, is nonetheless knowable without word revelation as being aesthetic in nature!

(§148) Later Schelling's interest will shift. He again starts with content, then comes the subject, the third, their unity, is the eternal.[95]

(§149) In the end, this triad of content, form, and schema is identified with the tri-unity immanent in the Godhead. The object or the content is called Father, the subject or the form is the Son, and the connection of both is the Holy Spirit.[96] By doing so, i.e., by exceeding the boundary [between God and the creature], the antinomy indeed recedes, but only to make room for the anomy.

(§150) Hegel is the philosopher of history, which he believes unfolds itself in an idealistic manner. He adopted the content of his system from Schelling, its process from Kant. Although metaphysics and logic first stand momentarily disconnected side by side, the monism of Schelling's metaphysics – which makes him much less individualistic than was Fichte – soon forged them together. Only the concept's form brings forth knowing's *generality*, hence in this genesis the absolute can be known mediately. For initially the absolute is unconscious reason, which becomes conscious of itself, and in it dialectical course first becomes idea, then nature, and finally spirit, and it attains its highest revelation in Hegel, the prophet.

(§151) Logic is the theory of the idea, the first phase. From *being*, without content and specification, are derived quality, quantity, and measure; out of *essence* appear the laws of thought [i.e., "essence as ground of existence"], appearance, and reality. The *concept* is the unity of being and essence that turns the parts into one whole. With respect to this concept one can distinguish the subjective concept, with its moments of passage, namely concept [as such], judgment, and syllogism, from the objective concept, which involves the trilogy: mechanism, chemical process, and

---

94   Kroner, *Von Kant bis Hegel*, II (Tübingen: Mohr [Paul Siebeck], 1924), 34.
95   Kroner, *Von Kant bis Hegel*, II, 108.
96   Kroner, *Von Kant bis Hegel*, II, 185.

teleological [/49] unity. The cancellation-through-elevation [*opheffing*; German: *Aufhebung*] of both, i.e., of the subjective and the objective concept, brings forth the idea as expressed in life, knowing, and the absolute idea.

(§152) In other words, this logic offers an ontological schema to which the idea remains bound, also in its operating outward in nature and in its return to itself in the spirit. Regarding this return, psychology takes precedence with the subjective spirit in its incipient moment as dreaming soul, in its ascent to reason, and in its completeness as intelligence and will; the two of which upon merging delineate freedom.[97]

(§153) In this way – I will not comment on this rather banal psychology – the *logos*, in the sense of the schema of logic, is very prominent. But the following [six] points are thereby overlooked. In the first place, this schema is an organon *only for the sciences*; per se it is no more than a cosmic interrelationship of distinct character. That this *logos*, with its categories of system, relation, and moments, can become the organon of science is due in part to its place in the cosmic order [i.e., as the first or least complex sphere], which determines its relation to the other spheres.

(§154) Hence, secondly, this schema is not as yet *ratio* [i.e., rationality in operation]: *ratio* always involves the connection of the subject with the logical schema.

(§155) Thirdly, *ratio* is prior to concept. Concept is the result of understanding, of grasping. This grasping presupposes not only mental activity but also something that comes to lie upon the schema in its forward movement, like soil scooped on the shovel as form.

(§156) In the fourth place, the motion involved in coming to understand is owing entirely to the subject. In contrast, if everything, including the logic of things, is in flux, as Hegel maintains, then *coming* to know requires nothing less than total rest. Truth's impetus would take us along with it like passengers sitting peacefully in a moving vehicle.[98]

---

97 K. Vorländer, *Geschichte der Philosophie*; Band II: *Philosophie der Neuzeit* (Leipzig: Meiner, 1919), 304–321.

98 See Rümelin's valuable description of the followers who fail to understand precisely this point and ask each other: "Do you understand it then? Does the concept move in you on its own and without effort on your part?" Gustav Rümelin, *Reden und Aufsätze* (Tübingen, 1875), 48, cited in (Ueberweg-)Oesterreich, *Die deutsche Philosophie des XIX Jahrhunderts und der Gegenwart*, 12th ed. (Berlin: Mittler & Sohn, 1923), 77. [/75]

(157) Fifth, not even understanding follows the way of dialectics; a claim that needs to be maintained as long as the meaning of "dialectic" is not clearly defined. Certainly, every moment of a system can in turn become a system, and thus encumber a more specific relation with its moments. If one calls this further penetration into the truth about one moment "dialectical" rather than "discursive," then this choice of terminology is downright regrettable. After all, "*dialegesthai*" [i.e., the root of "dialectic"] denotes *speech*, the exchange of thoughts between at least two persons.

(§158) Those who choose this word for the process of understanding take the bond between judgment and language to be a very close one. Plato's distinction between the two gets lost and one recedes to the standpoint of an archaic logic that confuses, as in Heraclitus, the speaking of prophesies with the forming of concepts.

(§159) Real prophets, however, are more apt to carefully distinguish the two. Not to mention that [/50] one can only question Hegel's speaking of the divine nature of a process that chose him as prophet!

(§160) Finally, language refers beyond itself, as do concepts; in that they do indeed agree. But that is their only point of agreement. Our discussion of nominalism,[99] however, made plain the dangers of confusing the two referents. For language lends its tongue to communicate both concepts and pseudo-concepts; it makes genuine knowledge public as well as wayward opinion. In other words, language offers no warrant for truth possession. Lacking another criterion one does well, like Cratylus, to choose silence. If one does speak, then one's words probably won't lack the power of suggestion – many skeptics were and are excellent orators – but what gets passed on is either doubt, which tears at one's own heart, or enthusiasm, which prevents drawing the skeptical consequences to which the theory of unstable truth must lead.

(§161) Hegel was anything but a skeptic. He created waves high with enthusiasm. But the skeptical attitude of mid-nineteenth century empiricists oriented to the inquiry of nature attests clearly both to the impotence of dialectics to prepare solutions for the problems that were then current as well as to the largely irrelevant joy of the romantic school.

5. *Some mid-nineteenth century figures*
(§162) Although the all too close connection between language and judgment was soon rejected, the connection between judgment and concept

---

99   See above §42.

was retained across the board – with one favorable exception, to which I shall return directly.

John Stuart Mill, who views all knowledge as perception recast by the "unifying ideas" of the mind, who speaks of "permanent possibilities of sensation" without distinguishing what is possible and what it is that makes possible, [and] who presupposes, in order to escape from solipsism, that the body of fellow creatures is an object of physics – him, with his associative induction[100] – I may surely pass by.

Hegel's most penetrating critic at the time was Adolf Trendelenburg.[101] In his *Logische Untersuchungen* Trendelenburg defends the Aristotelian connection of concept and perception on the one hand and the relationship of judgment and concept on the other. His follower Friedrich Ueberweg was in turn more sympathetic towards Hegel, at least in the period in which he designed his *System der Logik*. According to Adolf Lasson at least, Ueberweg's ontology at the time maintained: (i) that perception has to do with the being of time, space, force, and substance; (ii/iii) that sensibility and concept have to do with the being-for-itself [i.e., Hegel's *für-sich-sein*, cognitive awareness] of the individual, genus, essence, and appearance; and that (iv/v) judgment and syllogism hone in on the being-together of relation, causality, and goal.[102] During the preparation[103] of the next (1857) edition of his *System der Logik und Geschichte der logischen Lehren* Ueberweg's strange psychologically oriented thoughts seem to captivate him; thoughts which, needless to say, honestly display the foolishness of semi-idealism – he speaks of a space in which our representations are formed, which, since they are also extensive, are the representatives in the body of the world of appearances! [/51] Logic and the theory of knowledge are also obviously confused; logic is called the "science of the normative laws of human knowing" and proceeds in a concatenation of the five processes just mentioned: perception, sensibility, concept, judgment, and syllogism. In this way, perception is once again knowledge. It assumes intuition's position and thus, in being im-

---

100 A.K. Rogers, *English and American Philosophy since 1800: A critical survey* (New York: Macmillan, 1922), 64–86, especially 77–79.

101 Adolf Trendelenburg, *Logische Untersuchungen* I, 2nd ed. (Leipzig: Hirzel, 1862), especially in the third chapter, pages 36–129.

102 A. Lasson, "Zum Andenken an Fr. Ueberweg," *Philosophische Monatshefte* 7 (1871): 20, cited in F.A. Lange, *Geschichte des Materialismus und Kritik seiner Bedeutung in der Gegenwart*, II: *Geschichte des Materialismus seit Kant*, 9th ed. (Leipzig: Brandstetter, 1915), 490.

103 Lange, *Geschichte des Materialismus seit Kant*, 491.

mediate, acquires priority with respect to mediate thought.[104] The processes are of an internal psychical nature; one would hardly expect otherwise of a student of Friedrich Eduard Beneke.[105]

6. B. Bolzano

(§163) The only favorable exception, adumbrated above, is Bernard Bolzano. His epistemological thoughts rise far above those of his contemporaries, not only in disentangling judgment and concept but also in reaching back in his *metaphysics* behind idealism, including Kant's, to Leibniz. In *epistemology*, however, he has an almost isolated position. His *Wissenschaftslehre* [philosophy of science] makes a very sharp distinction between truth and knowledge,[106] and speaks there of independent statements, truths, and representations (*Sätze, Wahrheiten und Vorstellungen an sich*).

(§164) "Statement" [*Satz; stelling*] here should not be identified with a judgment, for a statement can be thought without being accepted.[107] The same holds with respect to the independent truths,[108] which in my opinion are somewhat more [complex] than the *lekton* ["the sayable"] of the Stoics and the *cogitationes possibiles* [possible thoughts] of Leibniz.[109] In every statement two representations or denotations are bound together as constituent parts, the sum of which is the content of the statement. If one replaces variable representations of a statement according to a specific rule with other [representations], then one can express the relation in which a set of such statements stands to the original [statement] in grades of validity.

(§165) Now, say one accepts for the moment that Bolzano's "*Sätze an sich*" are identical to concepts (in our terminology), and that his "*Vorstellung an sich*" more or less agrees with our moment of truth, then one

---

104 A. Döring, *Grundlinien der Logik als einer Methodenlehre universeller sachlicher Ordnung unserer Vorstellungen. Ein Versuch die Logik auf neuer Grundlage zu gestalten* (Leipzig: Meier, 1912), 11.

105 Oesterreich, *Die deutsche Philosophie des XIX Jahrhunderts und der Gegenwart*, 281–282.

106 B. Bolzano, *Wissenschaftslehre, Versuch einer ausführlichen und grössentheils neuen Darstellung der Logik mit steter Rücksicht auf deren bisherige Bearbeiter* I, 2nd ed. (Leipzig: Meiner, 1914; 1st ed. 1837), 62 ff. and 115 ff.

107 Bolzano, *Wissenschaftslehre* I, 77.

108 Bolzano, *Wissenschaftslehre* I, 111 ff.

109 H. Bergmann, *Das philosophische Werk Bernard Bolzanos, nebst einem Anhange: Bolzanos Beiträge zur philosophischen Grundlegung der Mathematik* (Halle: Niemeyer, 1909), 12.

immediately understands how epistemology was, in my opinion, honing in on important insights in Bolzano. All the more so since the distinction of judgment and thought that emerges here is not meant psychologically, and thus far transcends Descartes' distinction between *ideae* [ideas] and *iudicia* [judgments]. In this way one can distinguish simultaneously: to suppose [*menen*], to hold as true, and to assert, both as regards the grasping of truth in a specific form and as regards willing.[110]

(§166) One may perhaps remark that I am reading too many of my own opinions into Bolzano's thought. Historical research that goes deeper than I have been able to attain up to this point may indeed lead to the discovery of rather serious differences. So let me hasten to add that the agreement cannot be one of principles. Should it however continue to hold in light of further research, then it can only be explained as arising from the analysis of the same material. For the great obstacle hindering the development of epistemology was and continues to be the lack of analysis.

I am critical [/52] moreover not only of his metaphysics, designed according to Leibniz's model, but also of his confusing use of language. For while the agreement was so striking to me after reading only a little of his work – I surmise that some of his thoughts struck me because of the work of others, especially that of Edmund Husserl – the choice of terminology is certainly not a matter of indifference. Although I provisionally accepted Bolzano's "*Vorstellung an sich*" as agreeing with my use of "truth moment," his talk of "representation" ["*voorstelling*"] is nevertheless characteristic. That is why Bolzano cannot account for the place that negation and pseudo-concept have in knowledge. For instead of speaking of an unsuccessful concept formation – either in its not being completed or its being completed but yielding a pseudo-concept – Bolzano seeks solace in the use of the terms "existent" and "non-existent"; predicates that, in connection with the distinction of "existence" and "subsistence" ["*bestand*"], only too clearly expose the semi-idealistic tendency also of this system.[111] The same goes for the denial of truth character to *these* representations, which are certainly♦ more than representations, and the identification of individual representation and sensibility. Not to mention that in connection with "statement" ["*stelling*"], or being stated/posited, the divine "positor," who rests the circle of consideration on the *logos*, and the human "positor," who posited the field of inquiry in the logical form, are

---

110 Oesterreich, *Die deutsche Philosophie des XIX Jahrhunderts und der Gegenwart*, 185.
111 Bergmann, *Das philosophische Werk Bernard Bolzanos*, 55.

neglected.[112] Equally untenable is that space and time are said to be concepts on account of their not being taken as [forms of] sensibility!

(§167) We need to be reasonable and admit that it wasn't this kind of criticism that checked the acceptance of Bolzano's thoughts. Rather only [his] sensualism is guilty in this respect. Even the mathematicians noticed this, with the result that the Bohemian thinker's standpoint in mathematics,[113] known of quite early, was not appreciated.

7. *Other mid-nineteenth century figures*

(§168) In other areas it was exactly the same. The positive significance of discoveries between 1839 and 1850 by Theodore Schwann in biology and Robert Mayer in physics was given little attention. The focus fell rather on what they were distancing themselves from: namely, from vitalism in biology and the chemical view of heat [in physics]. In this way, support for untenable views was temporarily garnered from what might have contributed to drawing the proper boundaries of the circles of consideration for both of these disciplines, and eventually erupted in a conflict, conducted in a totally unphilosophical fashion on both sides, pro and contra materialism.

The vitalism of Rudolf Wagner included an Aristotelian epistemology and a supranatural view of faith, whereas Karel Vogt asserted that thoughts are to the brain as gal is to the liver and urine to the kidneys.[114] Gustav Fechner's metaphysics did not advance beyond an animism that was inspired by the natural philosophy of Lorenz Oken, which bound spirit and nature as inner and outer, and which in turn linked vitalistic [/53] panpsychism [*albezielingsleer*] to a mechanistic biology.

Rudolf Hermann Lotze deviates favorably from him by distinguishing within nature: laws, matter, force, and the original arrangement of what is material, the diathesis. But in the final analysis what we have here is no more than a connection of mechanism, albeit deepened, with idealism, namely, besides the kingdom of beings there is the realm of validity [*het geldige*], which contains both truths and values. As for his *logic*, he distinguishes, at the psychical level, representation and thought, and in

---

112 Bolzano, *Wissenschaftslehre* I, 77.

113 Cf. B. Bolzano, *Paradoxiën des Unendliches*, herausgegeben aus dem schriftlichen Nachlasse des Verfassers von Fr. Prihonsky, 2ᵉ ed (Berlin: Mayer & Müller, 1889).

114 Oesterreich, *Die deutsche Philosophie des XIX Jahrhunderts und der Gegenwart*, 268.

♦[Reading "zeker" for "zoeken" (search); A.T.]

each of these again act and content. While the connection of representations is controlled by the "happenstance" of the logical "mechanism," thought stands critically over against this. It separates representations whose connection is not legitimated by a right inherent in the nature of their contents out from representations where this is the case. Thought lets those connections be and reconstructs them in a new form in such a way that the right of the unity is clearly evident.[115] The forms and laws of thought are as much dependent on the material that has to be processed through them and according to them, as on the nature of those who will use them.[116]

If Lotze had now concluded that the form has a metaphysical bent, also when used by the soul, then his distinctions would have helped advance logic. But then he would also have rejected the idealistic identification of form, as viewed in the logical law-sphere, with "consequence of the organization of our subjective mind."[117] Now, since he does not do this, his rejection of the picture-theory [*afbeeldingstheorie*] amounts to throwing the baby out with the bathwater: the picture is not replaced by representation [*vertegenwoordiging*] and the cosmic law-sphere and truth about it are identified. In addition, the distinction of thought material (the representations) and its content crosses that of thought-form and material; in other words, the "content of thought" – accepting for a minute this terminology – is the transformed content of *representation*.

(§169) That is the error of all idealists. And I could break off my discussion of Lotze here were it not for the fact that he is the originator of the logic of validity. He speaks namely not only of statements [*stellingen*] but also of truths that hold [*gelden*].[118] Now it is indeed possible to say that a true judgment has a certain value, and as such may and can hold. But, first, this does not denote the distinctive characteristic of truth in the least – assuming that it could be described. If that were so, then an expression such as "truth holding" ["*geldende waarheid*"] would be a tautology. But that is not at all the case, as is evident when one reflects on the meaning of "holding." E.g., I can meaningfully say: "This judgment

---

115 R.H. Lotze, *Grundzüge der Logik und Enzyclopädie der Philosophie, Dictate aus den Vorlesungen*, 5th ed. (Leipzig: Hirzel, 1912), 6.

116 Lotze, *Grundzüge der Logik und Enzyclopädie der Philosophie*, 8.

117 Lotze, *Grundzüge der Logik und Enzyclopädie der Philosophie*, 8.

118 R.H. Lotze, *Logik, Drei Bücher vom Denken, vom Untersuchen und vom Erkennen*, etc., herausgegeben und eingeleitet von Georg Misch (Leipzig: Meiner, 1912), 513–515.; "Plato wanted to teach nothing other than what we go through above: the validity of truths. . ." (513).

is true, but it didn't hold yet" or "doesn't hold as yet." Such examples can illustrate, with respect to "*holding*," how something of value is always related to a subject that *acknowledges* this value, also when one prefers to reserve the expression for what rightly holds. Truth however does have a metaphysical connection with other terrains, but it is completely in-dependent of knowledge. Also [/54] when truth holds as a value, it still remains a truth about [something]. When language pulls these moments together, then, as for me, it says "holding with respect to" ["*gelding om-trent*"]. But the term "holding" is risky, precisely because there is always included a "holding for," if not a "holding according to"[119] a subject, and precisely the latter is incidental for the truth.

8. *Of the Marburgers: H. Cohen*

(§170) Lotze himself modestly stuck, as did Christoph Sigwart, to the first meaning [of "holding for"]. But the Marburgers took "holding" to be a "holding according to." Now my context does not allow me to dis-cuss more than one thinker of this interesting school. The most conse-quential person among them is undoubtedly Hermann Cohen.

(§171) Cohen's significance was greater than he realized. For although, in virtue of a skewed interpretation of Kant's writings, he thinks of himself as Kant's follower, Cohen in many ways counters him. And the changes that he introduces are often for the better.

(§172) The spirit of the Renaissance reveals itself perhaps in none of these modern thinkers more clearly than in him. The cosmos is synonymous with culture, and philosophy as science needs to point out a foundation for its [culture's] terrains. Science as a domain of culture is bound to the phenomena, other terrains can only be known in a non-scientific way. In connection with the *Begründung* [founding] of science, the philosopher proceeds from what is, i.e., what he finds as *qualitate qua* [how quality], namely mathematical natural science. Things are different in the areas of ethics and aesthetics, for a moral law presupposes the human being as law-giver.[120] The two terrains of *Sein* [being] and *Sollen* [ought] are

---

119 P.F. Linke, "Die Existentialtheorie der Wahrheit und der Psychologismus der Geldungslogik," *Kant-Studien* 29 (1924): 395–415.

120 H. Cohen, "Einleitung mit kritischem Nachtrag zur neunten Auflage" to F.A. Lange, *Geschichte des Materialismus* (Leipzig: Brandstetter, 1914), 98: "In the limits of historical anthropology one ought to acknowledge in a forthright way the animal nature of human beings and thereby the mechanism of causality. But there is still the parole: *the human being, as law-giver, ought to presuppose a moral law.* This is what is new in connection with concepts, namely that the *moral law* can be neither a *law of*

not typified according to their nature, but according to their presumed relation to the human being. So ethics is not taken to be a science of a specific circle of consideration, but the creation of moral laws. These laws themselves lie behind the terrain of *Sein* or *Dasein* [existence]. The human being first needs to exist before being able to bring forth these laws. So nature and morality do not lie parallel, each to be investigated by a science; rather at the level of the laws of the latter region [i.e., morality] lies not nature but science in the sense of the natural sciences. Both [moral laws and natural science] have in common their having been created by reason.

(§173) Now the philosopher of culture is not interested in how *Dasein*, which natural science investigates, arose. Of course here too idealism peeps through the cracks of the construct.[121] The spontaneity of thinking can be understood only in terms of the synthetic psychology of this system. It only makes sense to speak of this spontaneity when over against this activity, which itself swallows up the logical [sphere], there is the receptivity of the sense-organs. From a realist standpoint thought is never spontaneous, though it is active. That psychical activity is called "thinking" which, after having been directed, as intuition, to the logical factor, is now aided by this logical factor to find the truth about the non-logical terrains. E.g., in this way "the bio-*logical*" offers, with the help of the logical factor as moment, formed truth about the biotic.

The logical factor is [/55] never more than a moment of science, at least to the extent that it is bound to psychical activity. In Cohen it is its seed. I don't use this word here erroneously. For the logical factor, once it is identified with thought, derives from the latter a progressive character, which according to the realist it does not deserve. For methodical pursuit is then no longer the [figurative] journey that a human being makes over a rough terrain, where the path still needs to be cleared here and there with the help of the logical factor as organon; rather it [method] is to be compared with the shape [*gestalte*] of the plant, this being the plant as sprung forth from the seed (the logical factor) that encloses in itself the possibility of development. That is the meaning of *das Urteil des Ursprungs* [the judgment of the origin; literally: "the primal part of the

---

nature nor also a *law of history*, when these two manners of approach are thought as natural; but moreover it also cannot be a law of *God*." [Translation A.T.]

121 H. Cohen, *Kants Theorie der Erfahrung*, 4th ed. (Berlin: Cassirer, 1925), 17: "But these beings freely secure their ground exclusively in thought, just as science does this exclusively in reason."

primal jump"], as the first judgment of the laws of thought.[122]

(§174) But the so-called logic of this idealistic philosophy of culture is not only one-sidedly scientific, not merely logical and methodological idealism, it is even more limited. It borrows its so-called spontaneous method from *natural* science. Now it is undoubtedly one of the greatest services of the Marburg school that her representatives have acquainted themselves with the methodology of the *newer* [i.e., more current] natural science. Hence their system relates in this respect to [Kant's] *Critique of Pure Reason* as the scientific discoveries of J. Maxwell to A. Einstein relate to those of Galileo to I. Newton. But then it also is as one-sided as the judgment of many a specialist,[123] and this is taken to be more amiss of the philosopher than of the scientific expert.

(§175) But Cohen *cum suis* [and those with him] are to be blamed for more than just this. Besides granting great influence to a science that is in a state of historical development, one need also critique the underestimation of the complicated nature of its method. For this method *presupposes* in an order-theoretical sense the logical, number, space, time, motion, and energy, and as well as these being in a distinct arrangement such that the foundation of the analogies of the lower recur in the higher circles. By injecting all this into the bedding of the logical [sphere], one fails to appreciate this wealth. At the same time the logical far overflows its banks. No wonder that, after having swallowed up a part of metaphysics and of psychology, it can in turn appear to return these now drenched with activity;[124] i.e., not just the [logical] schema but also the asserted continuity of thought. Precisely for that reason I also don't need to discuss the derivation of the judgments of mathematics and natural science. The error does not lie here [with these disciplines] but in the foundation, in the so-called judgments of the laws of thought. Were one now to ask what induced Cohen to view the logical as flowing, then the answer can only be: the pleasure of finding a foundation, one that is not rational but nevertheless still active in a logical sense, for the creation of the ethical♦ and the aesthetic. In this way the *logos*

---

122 H. Cohen, *Logik der reinen Erkenntnis*, 2nd ed. (Berlin: Cassirer, 1914).

123 A.C. Elsbach, *Kant und Einstein: Untersuchungen über das Verhältnis der modernen Erkenntnistheorie zur Relativitätstheorie* (Berlin und Leipzig: De Gruyter, 1924). This author states quite correctly: "It cannot be the case that physics can be in conflict with Kantian philosophy, for their agreement is a necessary consequence of the structure of critical philosophy" (196). The question is whether this is an asset to be praised or a liability to be censured. [/76]

124 P. Natorp, *Hermann Cohens philosophische Leistung unter dem Geschichtspunkte des Systems* (Berlin: Reuther & Reichard, 1918), 29 ff.

is activated, namely refashioned according to the (also one-sidedly active) image of the human being.

(§176) However, science remains rational. That is why – rightly – the foundation disappears in perception. Thus space and time lose their status as forms of sensibility, however only to be resurrected in Hegel's spirit as – flowing – [/56] forms of thought. For there is only one object: nature. Thus the *Ding an sich* [thing in itself] is no longer, as with Kant, set aside *pro memorie* [so as not to forget], to be reminded of the possibility of the non-spatial temporary arranging of the contents of perception; rather it becomes the concept of the boundary of complete determination.

(§177) Though all this is more in a Hegelian spirit, the remarkable difference between Romanticism and Renaissance does still come through. The former accepts an ultimate closure of the process of knowing, the latter looks for this only in the identity of the method. Hegel is the rationalistic historian, who thinks that the development of the objective spirit in history becomes knowable to him. The Marburger is the methodologist of natural science. The *science* of history ought in the end to be physicalized.[125] On the other hand, history as process no longer falls under scientific knowledge, only under the creative *logos*. Paul Natorp maintains that to reflect on this process after having lived through it experientially is to do psychology.

9. Of the Freiburgers: H. Rickert
(§178) The so-called Freiburg approach [also known as the Baden school] presents a somewhat different picture. Its representatives share with the Marburgers the challenge of providing grounds for the form-content schema, and thus, like Fichte and Hegel, transcend Kant. Here too philosophy concerns itself with the sciences and not with their terrains; the peculiar uniqueness of these terrains is denied.

(§179) But there is a difference. Heinrich Rickert – here too I will limit myself to one typical figure – does not appeal to a single mathematical theme in connection with the active methodological *logos*.[126] In that way his whole way of thinking has a less technical cachet than that of Cohen. In addition he prefers to speak of norms, and in light of the current

125 Von Aster, *Neukantianismus und Hegelianismus*, 15–23.
126 H. Rickert, *Das Eine, die Einheit und die Eins*, 2nd ed. (Tübingen: Mohr [Siebeck], 1924), 87.

♦[Reading "ethische" for "aethetische" (*sic*); A.T.]

confusion of norm, command, and law his system readily appears to be less idealistic. One is so used to the dominance of mathematical natural science that, also in Christian circles, preference is often given, though usually without further reflection, to whoever dares to unburden himself of this yoke.

(§180) However, for that very reason, in my opinion, reflection is doubly called for.

(§181) Rickert proceeds from historiography, which became very prominent in the nineteenth century, not least of all under the influence of Romanticism in Germany, as names such as L. Ranke, T. Mommsen, and J. Burckhardt attest. Following W. Windelband's lead, Rickert now enquires into the logical presuppositions of history as science. As for historical description one can distinguish the evaluation and the result of inquiry. In the *description* these are always together. But what is the method of this science? He thinks he can mark out this method as being related to values that are secured in norms.[127]

(§182) Now one ought to object to this straightaway. Historical persons are not related to *values* but to their *task* and one does not investigate which values they realized but how they [/57] executed their task. Now a task is assigned and needs to be accepted; there must also be a view regarding it. But still it starts with an assignment that rests in the authority of the one sanctioned to assign these tasks. A *norm*, however, is not an assignment but a *measure*, and whether something has value can certainly be determined with the aid of such a measure. But norms are totally unsuited to secure values, unless one identifies value and its holding [*gelding*], or a good and its acknowledgement.

(§183) Secondly, Rickert's concept of value, which is really the heart of his view, is very vague. Legality [*recht*], the economic life, science, and religion are all listed as values. But these don't belong together at all, for legality and economic life are law-spheres, science is the execution of a task, and religion is the one side of a trans-cosmic connection. Grouping these four under the heading "value" is to be censured, but so is the "hypostatization" of the value concept. These four all *have* value or can again *acquire* it, but nothing in this list *is* value.[128] This must be strictly maintained, especially in connection with truth; for truth only acquires

127 H. Rickert, *Der Gegenstand der Erkenntnis: Einführung in die Transzendentalphiloso-phie*, 3rd ed. (Tübingen: Mohr [Siebeck], 1915), 366 ff.

128 V. Hepp, in *De waarde van het Dogma* (Kampen: Kok, 1920), states quite correctly: "Value rises and falls according to the need" (15).

value as anticipated possession, as knowledge.

(§184) In the third place, for that very reason the difference between nature and culture – a difference that certainly exists – is totally inadequate as a *division* of the whole. An evident reason is that such a classification doesn't allow everything to come into its own. E.g., suppose that one equates the ethical terrain with culture, then it is just as much a law-sphere as the physical is. But these two don't exhaust the number of law-spheres. And whoever bifurcates the sciences must be able to prove, negatively, that the additional law-spheres are not mutually independent and, positively, that they can be deduced from the initial two law-spheres! This holds not only for a division based on content but also for a division executed on formal grounds.[129]

(§185) If now it holds that every bifurcation does violence to the wealth of diversity, then what Rickert proposes does even greater violence to every realist division. For culture is not a law-terrain of any intersection through cosmic unities, but the execution of a task – or the result of such – in which the cosmic unity "humanity" appears as subject. That already indicates that culture does not coincide with morality [which is an intersecting law-terrain].

(§186) It is particularly difficult to see to what use epistemology could put such a division. E.g., where does the logical form belong? To nature or to culture? If one takes it to lie in the logical law-sphere, then it is certainly not to be reckoned with culture, for, on the contrary, the possibility of its having arisen is due in part to it. But even less so does this realist factor [i.e., the logical form] belong to nature, according to Rickertian opinion. The latter identifies the idealistically transformed facts [*werkelijkheid*] of the positivists with reality.[130] In that way truth gets catalogued as belonging to values [in the nature/reality – culture/value dichotomy].

(§187) This [cataloguing of truth] does shift the question [about where logical form belongs], but it doesn't come a stitch closer [/58] to resolving it. For, fourthly, the main division of values into contemplative and

---

129 H. Rickert, *Kulturwissenschaft und Naturwissenschaft*, 3rd ed. (Tübingen: Mohr [Siebeck], 1915), 17.

130 H. Rickert, *Die Grenzen der naturwissenschaftlichen Begriffsbildung: Eine logische Einleitung in die historische Wissenschaften*, 3rd and 4th ed. (Tübingen: Mohr [Siebeck], 1921), xvi: "Thus I characterize in what follows as factual or real [*wirklich oder real*] the material of distinct research that is not yet methodologically processed and neutral."

active[131] is also untenable. An important reason is that there where the psyche most certainly does play a role this division promptly leaves us in the lurch. For it is said to correspond with the distinction of asocial case and social person, with logical values in particular belonging to the former. Now while there is certainly contemplation when grasping the logical [schema], as soon as it is used as organon the psyche is active. Does truth thereby suddenly shift from an asocial matter to social person? And what ground is there for placing the logical [schema], even if only initially, with asocial values – where Rickert takes knowing to be identical with judgment[132] and thus takes knowing to be subject to norms? We'll let pass that one cannot appeal to a *norm* for knowing and coming to know – this not being the same as a demand! – prior to and outside of assessing [*de beoordeling van*] knowledge to be genuine or not when pronouncing a judgment.

(§188) Fifthly, *grouping* the sciences, as he does, is no more possible for them than for the law-spheres. The only thing that can be achieved is an arranging by way of [differences in] methodology. That is why Rickert's rejecting the one dual division in favor of another is in itself already naive.

(§189) Having accepted the possibility of such a division, matters only become worse when he thinks that he can find a principle of division on formal terrain. And finally his choice is then such that even a formalist in epistemology can find fault with it. To name just one thing: the science of nature and that of culture are set over against each other as generalizing and individualizing respectively.[133] Now the correlate of "general" is not "individual" but "special." But, in addition, the individual lies as moment – which may, through further concept formation, become a system – in a *specific* circle of consideration and thus can never serve to typify one of the two possible directions of concept formation on *all* terrains. When it comes to concept formation one distinguishes the complicating and the simplifying [*simplicerende (sic)*♦] direction. The route [of complication] that leads from the whole to the moments is however not generalizing

---

131 H. Rickert, *System der Philosophie I: Allgemeine Grundlegung der Philosophie* (Tübingen: Mohr [Siebeck], 1921), 348 ff.

132 Rickert, *Allgemeine Grundlegung der Philosophie*, 370 ff.

133 Rickert, *Kulturwissenschaft und Naturwissenschaft*, 60.

♦[The equivalent in English would be "simplicating." The two directions of method will later be called, more traditionally, "resolution and composition"; A.T.]

and the one in the opposite direction [of simplification] is not special-
izing. One can speak meaningfully of "general" and "special" only on
the basis of comparison, hence in this case comparison of two concepts
already formed. Thus Rickert confuses the simplification that takes place
on one of the routes of concept formation both with that which is special
– and is first discovered through comparison – and with that which is
individual, which appears in a specific circle of consideration.

(§190) But even with this approach he doesn't achieve what he wants
to achieve. "*Einmaligkeit*" [uniqueness] doesn't *typify* the historical in its
essence; it is more like the distinguishing mark of the moment when
something happens – this indeed doesn't repeat itself – as well as of that
which takes place in it.[134] And repetition likewise doesn't express the essence of what is physical, as one immediately realizes when [/59] simply
distinguishing technical use and the science of energy.

(§191) In all this Rickert defends opinions for which there is in the Marburg School no more place than for the founding of natural science, and
through it of *Sein* [being] in *Sollen* [ought], [opinions that are] probably the clearest indication of the difference in point of departure of the
two Neo-Kantian schools. [In particular,] in Rickert the logical schema
is originally not only form [being] but also norm, hence on his view:
demand [ought].

(§192) One may also mention an important trait of agreement between
the two schools, namely the creation of the moral law – for Rickert, of
norms – by the human being. For despite all the talk about the heteronomy of values, this doesn't in the least mean a breach with humanism; it only helps to illustrate more clearly the *individualistic* standpoint
involved. For it is the *individual* who meets the norm, viewed as *nomos*
[law], as the other. But that doesn't entail that it arises out of non-human
soil. Values stand as social norms above the individual, but the philosopher also has to ground these values in the "*reine Ich*" [pure Ego]. Although this Ego is said to be the kernel of the person[135] and, owing to the
confusion of "knowing of" with "knowing that" (that is evident in one
of Rickert's most recent publications), to be *conscious* of much, including
concept-formation, it can never itself fall under a concept.[136]

---

134 J. Thyssen, *Die Einmaligkeit der Geschichte, eine geschichtslogische Untersuchung*
(Bonn: Cohen, 1924), 9–27.

135 Rickert, "Von Anfang der Philosophie," 121–162, especially 132–142.

136 Rickert, "Von Anfang der Philosophie," 142.

(§193) Thus for Rickert, the form-content schema, viewed as the connection of active construction with that which is given immediately, has the final say. That the subject intuits the logical factor as such, thus apart from the role that it plays as organon, does not even occur to him as a possible solution. Intuition [*schouwen*] is [here] simply the same as sensibility [*aanschouwen*]. Place beside this statement a second premise, namely the well-known saying of Kant: "Intuitions [*Anschauungen*] without concepts or content without forms are 'blind,'" and the conclusion is formally correct: "By merely intuiting [*bloszes Schauen*] one cannot as yet *theoretically* 'see,' which is to say: not *acknowledge* anything."[137] Thus also Rickert calls for a concept of the concept, the result of the attempt to resolve a problem before it is well-formulated.

10. F. Brentano and E. Husserl

(§194) We found that both Cohen and Rickert affirm that "knowing is fashioning by thought what is intuitively sensed." Does Husserl have anything else to offer? The question is intentionally formulated in this [limited] way, for this thinker has introduced too many distinctions than allow for even a partially adequate discussion of his thought.

(§195) In answering this question let us try to advance historically by paying attention to his teachers.

(§196) Then Brentano is the first to attend to. He is oriented in an anti-Kantian way to Descartes and Leibniz,[138] with philosophy focused above all on evidence. Although mathematical concepts are adopted from experience, mathematical judgments are immediately evident; i.e., they are not based on induction (as are the judgments of physics); for, contrary to Aristotle, induction is here reduced to a calculus of probabilities.[139] In

---

137 Rickert, *Das Eine, die Einheit und die Eins*, 85. [Vollenhoven appears to quote Kant as cited by Rickert. The quote should read: "Thoughts without content are empty, intuitions without concepts are blind." I. Kant, *Kritik der reinen Vernunft*, A 51/B 75. I add that in Vollenhoven "schouwen," which is intuitive viewing, is much broader than the "intuition" of "Anschauung," which operates at the level of sensibility. This also gives to concepts a different role than that of making blind intuitions "see"; A.T.]

138 F. Brentano, *Versuch über die Erkenntnis*, Aus seinem Nachlasse herausgegeben von A. Kastil (Leipzig: Meiner, 1925), 3–48.

139 F. Brentano, *Psychologie vom empirischen Standpunkt*, II: *Von der Klassifikation der psychischen Phänomene*, mit ausführlicher Einleitung und Register herausgegeben von O. Kraus (Leipzig: Meiner, 1925), 50–53. [The 2nd and 3rd lines from the bottom of page 59 have been interchanged, thereby correcting the text to read: "wijl ze, hoewel de wiskundige begrippen aan ervaring zijn ontleend, anders dan die der

this way Brentano again avails himself of the old distinction [/60] of eternal and contingent truths but in a new way. Later, as does Wolff, he drops this in the conviction that what Leibniz posed as his task, he, Brentano, has executed. The principle of sufficient reason is said to be reduced to the *principium identitatis* [principle of identity].

(§197) Despite his protest Brentano is to be reckoned with the psychologizers [*psychologisten*] in the sense that he incessantly confuses epistemological, logical, and psychological divisions. However, this is not to say that there is no value in what he found. First of all, one can appreciate the statement that everything that is psychological intends, i.e., has something to which it refers. Secondly, on that basis he rejects every classification of things psychical that is derived from the intended referent. Put positively, in his opinion, one ought to search for its principle [of division] in the manner in which the intended referent is viewed by the psyche. As possible ways of bringing to view he proposes: representation, judgment, and loving with hating. Brentano drew two conclusions from this grouping that proved to be productive for epistemology: (i) there is a sharp incision between judgments and representations, and (ii) likewise a similar incision between judgment and concepts. Here [(ii) follows from (i) because] Brentano reckoned concepts with representations. The latter point puts him at odds with *inter alios* the Marburgers; but also with the Freiburgers, given the way he links value to the phenomena of love and hate, which entails separating truth and value.

(§198) Nevertheless, here too our critical stance may not let up for a moment. I cannot address here whether the division he proposes for psychical phenomena actually remains unaffected by differences between intended referents, i.e., whether main divisions and subdivisions get mixed up here – that is a question for psychology to answer. But in epistemology too Brentano's position is vulnerable. For while he maintains that perception is judgment-like in character – thus confusing perception and judgments of perception – he also places concept and representation on a par, as if the organon of concept formation belongs to matters psychical! Precisely because of this misunderstanding of the relation of the psychical and the logical, the thought that what is non-real [*het niet-reëele*] cannot *be represented as* unreal [*irreëel*] is much too vague. That it cannot be known is of course correct, but this rests on totally different grounds than

---

physica niet steunen op inductie, die in afwijking van Aristoteles herleid wordt tot waarschijnlijkheidsberekening." A.T.]

the impossibility of representing something as being unreal.[140] For much is not imaginable to which reality should not in the least be denied, and thus "being imaginable" and "reality" are not congruent.

(§199) On the other hand, another more agreeable point is the further development of his theory of judgment, which refuses to wring all judgments in the schema of "S is P." For there are existential judgments [*existentiaal-oordelen*] of the form "A is." The schema "A is B" presupposes a synthesis of the *judgments*: "S is" and "P is." This synthesis does not arrange P with S, after having encumbered S with A and P with B, but it arranges the predicate *judgment* ["B is"] with the subject *judgment* ["A is"].[141] [/61]

(§200) But finally, the linking of representation and concept spoils everything. Thought may indeed be something other than judging; but knowing and judging remain on a par [for Brentano], just as the thing, in the Aristotelian sense of the word, is taken to be an essence-bound object of perception. These two [assumptions, about knowing and things] are compatible only when preserving both [with respect to the thing] the form-material schema, applied to the simplest judgments and the representations, and [as regarding knowing] the act-content schema, applied to the intention and the intended referent, according to which the form remains psychically active. Georg Misch, who notes that there is kinship between these thoughts and those of Lotze,[142] is as correct as Rickert is, when the latter reduces his difference with Brentano regarding the form-content dualism to a mutual divergence in terminology.[143]

(§201) After this excursion I now return to Husserl. His strong dependence on Brentano is limited to his first period,[144] during which, after completing his dissertation *Ueber den Begriff der Zahl, psychologische*

---

140 F. Brentano, "Zur Lehre von Raum und Zeit," *Kant-Studien* 25:1 (1920): 1–23, especially page 7.

141 F. Brentano, *Von der Klassifikation der psychischen Phänomene*, 77-81. [This approach was part of Brentano's reform of logic, especially the theory of judgments. Peter Simons notes, in "Brentano's reform of logic": "The basic idea of his theory of judgement was that the logical form of simple judgements is that of an assertion or denial of existence, rather than the subject-predicate form of the tradition"; P. Simons, *Philosophy and Logic in Central Europe from Bolzano to Tarski*, chapter 3 (Dordrecht: Kluwer, 1992), 41. A.T.]

142 G. Misch, in his introduction to H. Lotze, *Logik* (Leipzig: Meiner, 1912), xvi.

143 Rickert, *Das Eine, die Einheit und die Eins*, 85.

144 E. Husserl, "Erinnerungen an Franz Brentano," in: O. Kraus, *Franz Brentano, Zur Kenntnis seines Lebens und seiner Lehre* (München: Beck, 1919), 153–167.

Analysen (1887), he published *Philosophie der Arithmetik* [volume I, 1891]. In this work, when it distinguishes concept and number, intentionality has the final say, for any [natural] number aims to indicate not the concept of things, but the totality of their quantity. While undoubtedly correct as regards the naming of numbers, this approach nonetheless clearly fails to grasp the modality of number. As a result – although his remark that arithmetic does not work with genuine number concepts[145] is on the track of the notion of analogy – the analogies of the arithmetical field in the fields [of inquiry] resting on it cannot be assessed for their proper value, but are called "symbols."

(§202) But his *Philosophy of Arithmetic* brought some serious difficulties to a head, because, in mathematics in particular, Brentano's theory of abstraction [which Husserl availed himself of], had little to offer. This critique does not mean to infer a break-away from the confusion of *logos* and *ratio*. For, while searching for a dependable guide, Husserl did discover Bolzano.[146]

About 1896, the basic contours of the first part of Husserl's *Logische Untersuchungen* saw the light of day,[147] with its *deductio ad absurdum* [reduction to an absurdity] of all individualistic psychologism. Historically this made an enormous impression in the academic literature. But one exaggerates the significance of this work when presuming that it put an end to all psychologism – the simple fact that Husserl himself (in the introduction to the second volume, which he wrote after having finished volume 2, that is, after having achieved in it the greatest clarity) refers to his phenomenology as "descriptive psychology"[148] is telling. Several years later he himself challenged this formulation; but the grounds on which he demonstrates this to be in error only serve to offer a glimpse of the naïveté of his view of psychology. For that inner and outer perception have the same epistemological value is just as correct as the other assertion of Husserl, namely, that he had himself already realized this. But this [/62] does not yet prove that phenomenology is free of psychology, or the described *logos* of the *ratio*.

Now Husserl does distinguish, in connection with knowledge, the

---

145 E. Husserl, *Philosophie der Arithmetik, psychologische und logische Untersuchungen* I (Halle-Saale: Pfeffer [Stricker], 1891), 211–215.

146 Cf. above §§163–167.

147 E. Husserl, *Logische Untersuchungen*, I: *Prolegomena zur reinen Logik*, 2nd ed. (Halle: Niemeyer, 1913), xii.

148 Husserl, *Logische Untersuchungen*, II, 1: *Untersuchungen zur Phänomenologie und Theorie der Erkenntnis*, 2nd ed. (Halle: Niemeyer, 1913), 18.

psychical coherence, the connection in the state of affairs that is known, and the logical coherence. And while I too admit that this threefold schema is amazingly insightful, it does not thereby put an end to the confusion of *logos* and *ratio*.[149] That happens only when one satisfies the following conditions. (i) All that is other [than what is logical], hence also that which is psychical or arithmetical, must remain excluded from the logical [law-sphere]; the analogy of the logical is in every [non-logical] law-sphere, but nothing of these latter spheres is in the former. (ii) One should derive from this *logos* the schema with the help of which one can track down the analogy of the logical [law-sphere] in the remaining law-spheres; hence all activity should be absent from this schema – which is not to say that it cannot be used. (iii) Since a concept can only arise by connecting this schema as form with the analogy of the logical in a distinct circle of consideration as content, a concept of this schema cannot be had. It can only be viewed intuitively [*geschouwd*], for otherwise one is saddled with a concept of a concept, in other words, with a *regressus ad infinitum* [unending regression].

(§203) Husserl did not meet any of these conditions. He distinguishes "categories of reference" ["*Bedeutungskategorien*"] and "categories of *Gegenstand*" ["*Gegenstandskategorien*"] [i.e., categories of objective meaning].[150] Had he taken the difference between these to parallel the distinction between knowledge and truth, or truth and circle of consideration, then only a certain one-sidedness would be challenged here. But the pallid concept of *Gegenstand* again fades away the boundaries between thought and circle of consideration, as does also the ambiguous concept of *Bedeutung* between that of activity and content-seeking form. As a result, the threefold schema of act-form-content is soon forced into the background by the twofold and incomplete schema of act and content.[151] This causes a shift in all the members. First of all the form becomes active. But the content also, even though it continues to be called *gegenständlich* [objective], becomes formal on account of being clamped in by all the circles of consideration. That the form is active Husserl has in common with idealism; content's "formality" touches on scholasticism, with its identification of order-theoretical apriority and the generality of concepts.

---

149 D.H.Th. Vollenhoven, "Enkele grondlijnen der kentheorie," *Stemmen des Tijds* 15 (1926), 380–401.

150 Husserl, II, 1: *Untersuchungen zur Phänomenologie und Theorie der Erkenntnis*, 95 ff.

151 Husserl, *Logische Untersuchungen*, II, 2: *Elemente einer phänomenologischen Aufklärung der Erkenntnis*, 2nd ed. (Halle: Niemeyer, 1921), 1 ff.

Both active form and formal *Gegenstand* now require filling. The first acquires its filling from the intuitive intending [*aanschouwend intenderen*], which, although he does not always keep this clearly separate from matters perceptual, Husserl insists is not perceptual.[152] For example, he uses images adopted from perceptual focusing to clarify the categorical "filling in." This is risky. For suppose I see in the distance something with stem and branches and leaves, then I'm likely to say: "That is a tree." But I'll need to approach closer before it will be possible for me to decide what kind of a tree I'm dealing with. But this "approaching" is different from what happens in concept formation, which does not begin with "tree" but with "this, which is concrete"; in other words, it begins where phenotypical classification ends. For knowledge concerns the field [of inquiry] and the more specific categorial determination of the moment in this field. And the derivation of this tree from [/63] two other [genetic] factors, which I need in order to be able to know it, is something other than adjusting the focus of the perceptual image "tree" to discern it to be a "poplar."

This confusion of knowing and perceiving[153] is doubly costly for Husserl. For in Cartesian fashion he wants to exclude questions regarding "factual reality" ["*werkelijkheid*"][154] and hence makes it impossible for himself to distinguish perception and representation other than by way of the psyche [*over den psychischen weg*]. [...]♦ of a non-efferent moment, which is compatible with the psychological concept of act, but not with that of the idealistic theory of knowledge. The connection of the general act with that of the categorial "filling" takes place in the so-called act of identifying. Hence, in this way of thinking, general and particular are not intuited order-theoretically or/and as a distinction between moments of truth in two or more concepts found through comparison; no, the general is in the subject as possibility over against reality as "the filling." Thus the act-content schema here intersects with that of form-material. This is also applied to the cosmic order of the circles of consideration, and then in turn brought to bear in connection with necessity and contingency.

---

152 Husserl, II, 2: *Elemente einer phänomenologischen Aufklärung der Erkenntnis*, 128–164.

153 W. Ehrlich, *Kant und Husserl, Kritik der transcendentalen und der phänomenologischen Methode* (Halle-Saale: Niemeyer, 1923), 50 ff.

154 W. Moog, *Die deutsche Philosophie des 20 Jahrhunderts in ihren Hauptrichtungen und Grundproblemen* (Stuttgart: Enke, 1922), 252 ff.

♦[Missing words in the printed text; A.T.]

The question that remains is how the formal *Gegenstand* gets to be filled. When Husserl gets to this point he often remains silent. Sometimes he speaks of a correlation between *Gegenstand* and act, at other times it comes down to shaping [*vorming*].[155] The one need not be in conflict with the other, and both fit snugly in the intuitionist image of the life-stream,[156] that Husserl too is fond of.

(§204) This brings me to the last condition, namely the correct determination of the role of the intuition. According to the phenomenologist, it does not direct itself to the modality of the circle of consideration [*gezichtsveld*] nor, when preparing for concept formation, to the schema in the logical factor in particular, but to essences in a nonmetaphysical but logical sense. The turn towards the subject cannot be denied here either: the intuition directs itself especially to acts consciously undertaken [*doorleefde Akte*]. That already indicates that inner perception and epistemological intuition – [the latter as] thinking/supposing [*het menen*] – are being confused. But, in addition, the desperate activation of the form brings with it that Husserl thinks this is a viable way to come to a viewing [*schouwen*] of the logical schema and of the basic laws of logic. This viewing is certainly possible, but doing so then requires consciously working with the form as organon and not a [mere] reflecting on those efforts.

(§205) And so, the answer to the question whether Husserl advances a view of knowing that is different from that of idealism is a negative one [cf. §194]. Although there are instances where new trends do surface, he could not wrest himself away from the influence of idealism, neither the modern nor the older type. Thus he gets no further than a wavering between the self-intuition of the creative Ego and the biologistic phenotype epistemology of scholasticism.

(§206) Thus Hegel and Thomas Aquinas, idealism and semi-idealism, wrestle also in Husserl for the victory.[157] [/64]

11. *Epistemological forecast*

(§207) This sort of wrestling will continue to be the case for others as long as they fail to distinguish clearly between perceiving and knowing, [i.e.,] the phenotypical comparison of forms and the conceptual inquiry

---

155 Ehrlich, *Kant und Husserl*, 79, 155.

156 Husserl, II, 1: *Untersuchungen zur Phänomenologie und Theorie der Erkenntnis*, 343 ff. [/77]

157 E. Przywara, "Thomas oder Hegel, zum Sinn der 'Wende zum Object,'" *Logos* 15 (1926): 1–20.

of fields of inquiry on the one hand, and the psychical and the *logos*, [i.e.,] the activity of thinking and the form with which it works on the other hand. Anyone who has studied the most recent representatives in epistemology on these points knows that that is not the case for people like J. Volkelt and H. Driesch, N. Hartmann and S. Nuzubidse, J. Geyser and M. Scheler. And yet these basic distinctions must be considered vital; the gain undoubtedly booked in the details is secondary.

I. *A personal word*

(§208) For the time being, ladies and gentlemen, I will break off my inquiry at this point. For it is not critique, but only positive [*thetisch*] work that can in the long run break the power of the double tradition [of idealism/humanism and scholasticism] that hinders the free development of epistemology without at the same time inflicting the irreparable damage that is suffered repeatedly when one turns one's back to the old without having anything better to put in its place.

(§209) If, however, owing to a wrongheaded conservatism, one fails to seriously confront the demand to free the theory of knowledge of these powers, then sooner or later a synthesis of Christendom and one or another branch of humanism will emerge, and we will turn again down the fatal path that leads to the abyss. That was not only the experience of Christendom in the conflict that flared up between followers of Augustine and Thomas prior to the Reformation of the 16th century, but Reformed life can attest to this as well, also in our own country.

In our case there were various contributing factors. First of all, while people were enjoying the added privileges that accompanied a legitimate freedom of conscience, education was for the most part, questionably, left in the hands of the state. Its administrators soon drew their wisdom from thinkers who were unfamiliar with God's Scripture-revelation. Soon the graduates of higher education were being nurtured in the same direction by men of similar spirit, with predictable results. When it came to crossing swords with modern philosophy, the Reformed man of science was more at a loss than the common people. Because the intellectual milieu that Reformed academics inhabited was the same as those who opposed them, the conflict between them came down to a scuffle between conservative and progressive rationalism. People failed to see that in the premises of their own statements they had already granted what should above all have been denied. In that way the inheritors of the Renaissance [i.e., the humanists] easily booked one success after the other, while their initial opponent had to admit their inferiority.

Then – and that proved to be our good fortune – humanism became overconfident, annulled the compromise, and robbed the Christian part of the nation of its privileges. This not only incited this group
to greater activity, but also in particular led Groen van Prinsterer and
Abraham Kuyper in particular to a study of the foundations [/65] of
this compromise. Credit is due especially to Kuyper, not so much because he stood in the breach for what was oppressed, but because he
taught our people to freely relinquish established privileges. In so doing
he rejected both the supremacy of the state over the religious life of individuals and the thought that the state was the training school for morality and religion. In that way he broke not only with ancient Aristotle
but also with the Christianized [Aristotelianism] of the Middle Ages.

When inquiring as to what it was that brought Kuyper to act in this
way, the answer cannot be the tactics of withdrawing his men, distancing them from the enemy, so that soon a better blow could be delivered.
The basis of his procedure was not practical but theoretical: sphere sovereignty became his controlling maxim. True, he referred to both the cosmic unity [i.e., individuals and institutions] and the [modal] law-spheres
as "spheres." But his refusal to place the Church in the pyramid of the
law-spheres evidences, better than anything else, how a distinguishing of
these two [i.e., the cosmic determinants of individuality and modality] is
entirely consistent with the [main] line of his thought. But it also shows
how desperately blind all "anti-papism" is that combats Kuyper and his
followers in favor of a practical-political stance, all the while thinking
that they are doing God a favor by returning to the worldview of – of all
people – Thomas Aquinas.

(§210) While the conflict for the freedom of the Church broke the still
formative but lingering after-effects of scholasticism, the struggle for religious and spiritual freedom for all was directed more against the spokes-
men of the classical ideal. Even though Kuyper's thought flirts here with
Romanticism, by subjecting of all creation to the authority proper to different terrains and by acknowledging the high but limited task of science,
it is evident here too that these two meet merely in a practical sense, each
with its totally distinct point of departure, compass and route. ◆

(§211) Part of the Reformed approach [*conceptie*] was the demand for
freedom of education, including higher education. Borne by that intuition of reality that never seems to give way for the Calvinist, Kuyper
never confused ideal and reality. Also in these matters he acknowledged

on the basis of God's election not the duality of truth of course, but that of science.[158] The connection of the theory of sphere sovereignty with the practical acceptance of the duality in the human race increasingly gave credence to the plan of establishing this university, whose conception and growth is thus most intimately connection with both that theory and this humble bowing before God's order.[159]

(§212) That philosophy and especially epistemology were not overlooked at this institution – to limit myself here to those deceased – is evident also from the life of one like J. Woltjer, whose interest was especially focused on language as the vehicle of thought, but no less on divine revelation as it is known from the work of God's hands [*"werkstuk"*]. Particularly this second part of his inquiry brought him into contact [/66] with the difficulties of the theory of knowledge.

Already in 1895, in part for the sake of the theory of knowledge, a program was developed[160] whose content bore entirely both his signature and – to remain silent in connection with one still in our midst would be an historical injustice – also that of my immediate predecessor and mentor [W. Geesink]. That program states that "before all else it is likewise necessary to elicit answers from these (Reformed) principles to the questions that became more prominent only after Kant's inquiry into *the knowing subject*, i.e., to (the full implication of) questions that occurred to no one in the sixteenth century and thus also not to Calvin." While it is true that no connection is laid between a theory of knowledge and the principle of sphere sovereignty, a little further on the report straightforwardly resumes: "Yet according to Article 2 (of the Statutes of the

---

158 Kuyper, *Encyclopaedie der Heilige Godgeleerdheid*, II: *Algemeen deel*, 2nd ed. (Kampen: Kok, 1909), 97–132.

159 A. Kuyper, *Souvereiniteit in eigen kring*. Rede ter inwijding van de Vrije Universiteit den 20sten October 1880 gehouden in het Koor der Nieuwe Kerk te Amsterdam (Amsterdam: Kruyt, 1880), especially pages 17, 18.

160 [J. Woltjer and A. Kuyper], *Publicatie van den Senaat der Vrije Universiteit in zake het onderzoek ter bepaling van den weg die tot de kennis der Gereformeerde beginselen leidt* (Amsterdam: Wormser, 1895), 13–14.

◆ [Vollenhoven appears to have the Reformation's appeal to creation, word-revelation, and spirit-guidance respectively in mind here. This hovers in the background of §94. (It is made explicit in *Isagôgè Philosophiae* 1930/1931: §§72–78.) Romanticism has its own alternative view; see §100 for the Renaissance's preview of the same. These terms also have an inward application as categories of scientific method, namely, as field of inquiry, direction of simplification or complication, and adequate concept respectively; see §§137, 189; A.T.]

Association for Higher Education on a Reformed Foundation), answers to these questions, too, shall not be expected from elsewhere, but *must* be derived from the Reformed principles."

In this way, as regards this discipline, the older generation learned through trial and tribulation – note the year◆; but at the same time it postulated in faith the possibility of a theory of knowledge that does not turn faith away at the threshold, but that also needs to do full justice to knowledge, including the knowledge of scriptural revelation. The conviction that this possibility can be realized is entailed in the foundation of the critique implied in the historical overview presented to you this afternoon.

Honored Directors of our Association and Curators of this university
(§213) That your boards called me to the high office that I accepted this afternoon has filled me with great gratitude towards God, who, from the time of my youth, wanted to be a Father, teaching me from out of the Scriptures and detaining me when I wanted to wander, and who held me when I grew faint. Also, in the area of science, he not only let me search through struggle but also prepared me graciously to find the joy that, as I hope, will bring honor to his name. At this moment in particular I thank him that early this summer, under his guidance, your attention turned to me and you granted me your trust.

(§214) But I am also thankful to you that from the moment of my appointment you approached me with greater benevolence than I had dared to expect. Therefore I convey to you quite frankly the joy that was in my heart when the opportunity presented itself for me to dedicate myself completely to the academic interests that so captivated me that I simply couldn't pass this by even for the sake of the work that is so satisfying in the very flourishing church of The Hague-West. Connecting the depth of my study of an area that is sometimes quite far removed from [/67] pastoral care with my empathizing in the struggle of faith of both the healthy and the sick became easier, in a principled way, to the extent that the light of Scripture fell more clearly both on persons in their need, whether living or dying, as on theories generated by the heart of persons who are in essence similar. But time and fortitude were limited; accordingly, your appointment resolved the great tension in which I have lived

---

◆ [Vollenhoven probably has in mind the conflict around A.F. de Savorin-Lohman and his use of the Reformed principles. He was a member of the university staff and was discharged in 1895; A.T.]

the last years.

(§215) That the move – difficult as it was – away from the court capital [The Hague] did not mean a lasting break in my very fruitful contact with Dr. H. Dooyeweerd, whom you called to this university simultaneously with me, increased my joy appreciably.

(§216) I intend, with the power and grace that God grants me, to carry out with complete dedication the task you have placed on my shoulders. May it be: (i) for the formation of fresh troops, which will constantly be needed to maintain ourselves in the old battle that currently must be fought on very uneven terrain; (ii) for deepening the distinction between what is truly a matter of principle and what simply arose in connection with practical circumstances; (iii) for reuniting – naturally not through compromise but as a matter of conviction – what individualism, in the previous century and also again in this century, has broken asunder; (iv) and, above all, for the glory of him who sees our struggle and whose faithfulness will not tolerate our defeat so long as we only keep his Word.

Esteemed Professors!
(§217) Your circle consists for a good part of those to whom, having been my teachers, I owe a great debt of gratitude for what you have meant to me through personal contact and through your instruction in lectures and books. To see you now as colleagues is not without its awkwardness. However, my recollection of those years when my relationship to you was otherwise is my warrant that you will gladly help me by sharing with me your experience.

Others of you became or were through personal acquaintance or agreement in age my friends and fellow students. I need merely ask of you to carry on in this regard, now strengthened by the "esprit de corps" in the noblest, religiously hallowed sense of the word.

In turn, I came into contact with a third group scattered among those gathered here because your area of interest intersected with that of my research. Let me assure you that, because they [. . .]◆ spur me on, I will continue to wrestle with many a difficult question found by the light of the Holy Scripture.

(§218) I thank you for the cordiality all of you have extended to me – in one case, at a very difficult time for me, there was an act of mercy. Please accept my promise of collegial faithfulness and cordial cooperation – in

---

◆[Missing portion of the text; A.T.]

light of my subjects of teaching and research one would expect no less. [/68]

Highly Esteemed Geesink
(§219) The "*rude donatus*" [honorable discharge], which appeared for the first time behind your name on the lecture roster this year, must be difficult for you, who already in my student days gladly would tarry in the circle that pleased you. May it be satisfying for you that several persons are required to bear the load that up to now was assigned solely to you. Now in connection with your philological lectures in particular: in one of your sermons, which your students are fond of reading, I recently came across your definition in-passing of worldly wisdom: "maintaining that the sensory-perceptible world is more real than the spiritual-cognitive one."[161] Well now, be convinced that I shall never teach your former students *Weltweisheit* [philosophy; lit. "world wisdom"] in this sense. And since you equally have no sympathy for the other extreme of placing the emphasis on the reality of the spiritual-cognitive at the expense of the reality that is proper to the sensory-perceptible, you may be confident that in this connection the old line will be followed. May you be richly blessed in the autumn of your life, knowing also that the continuity of your work in many ways is ensured.

Respected Brothers, representatives of the Churches of 's Gravenhage [i.e., The Hague]
(§220) It was only a short while ago that I took leave of you – hopefully not for good! The many things I experienced in your midst and in the congregation were already mentioned when parting. Now, on this occasion, I want to thank you in particular for always having allowed me to work in the way I saw fit, apparently in the conviction that each person achieves the most when allowed to proceed at his own pace. That will remain with me, not just as a pleasant memory but also as an example in the contact with those persons whom I will soon help prepare for their spiritual and largely also ecclesiastical, task.

Dear Students: Ladies and Gentlemen
(§221) Giving myself to you in contact and instruction will from now on not only be a duty; on the contrary, also a privilege. By contact, which I place in the foreground, I mean not only the hours intentionally devoted

---

161 W. Geesink, *De nederigen vertroost, twaalf preeken* (Amsterdam: Gebroeders Binger, 1908), 36.

to conversation; those, after all, are but few in number, for you and I are also going to have to work hard.

(§222) In choosing this sequence I want to emphasize, however, that I always hope to bear in mind, also during my personal study and teaching, that there is still something more than science: our *life*. To be sure, that life, since everything created rests on the *logos*, is not a-logical; but it is irrational. It owes its being and becoming to God, who, according to his order of things, has seen fit for you to experience this day and age in which [/69] modernity is discerning the disruption of *its* life. If you are simply children of this age, then with some cultivation of self-reflection you will be able to live through this fragmentation intensely and maybe later also describe it movingly. But surely there is something better to do with *our* life. We are children of a generation that – even though we may have felt that death came too soon – knew how to die in grace, after having brought forth something great through its obedient confidence in the God of the covenant. For us to criticize their work here or there – we who first plucked the fruits and now only have to argue about what could have been – is probably not difficult. But none of us is entitled to do so who has not first, as did they, bowed ever more deeply before the elevated God. Whoever does this, also among you, discerns one's future *task*, namely of avoiding all dangerous self-presumption, and in heart-felt cooperation with whomever one finds at one's side in whatever life-connection to overcome that so humanistic individualism of person and [life-]sphere and, on every terrain where one is called by God, to work towards the same ideal as stirred the hearts of the ancestors.

(§223) I urge you to prepare yourselves especially for the struggle against that individualism.

(§224) In that connection philosophy will be a handicap so long as you, like Pascal, might be under the impression that the God of Abraham, Isaac, and Jacob is not the same as the God of philosophers and academics. But philosophy could be useful for you if and when you subject your whole life, also your thinking, lovingly and thus in obedience, to him, who also binds you to himself.

(§225) He brought us together.

(§226) That is why I want to see my task and your task always bound together in that twofold mighty word full of genuine religion: "I will proclaim the Name of the LORD. Oh, praise the greatness of our God!" [Deuteronomy 32:3].

Translator's Postscript

On 18 November 1938 the curators of the *Vrije Universiteit* received a formal complaint from the theological faculty charging Vollenhoven with departing from the Reformed confessions on two points: (i) the denial of "the duality of human existence, namely as a material, mortal body and as a immaterial, immortal soul"; and (ii) the denial that God's Son had "an impersonal human nature" ("*anhypostatos*") – the contrary view of God's Son having a "personal" human nature, as held by Vollenhoven, was considered to be "an error reminding one of Nestorius."[1]

The first point is confused. Vollenhoven never denied the distinction of body and soul. What he did criticize is the way the distinction is drawn and defended in the Protestant scholastic tradition. (This tradition is still influential today.) A separate committee was formed to look into the matter. But the second world war intervened, and the matter was dropped.

The second point is based on a passage in Vollenhoven's *Calvinism and the Reformation of Philosophy*, which is unfortunately vague and thus capable of being read as (possibly) "Nestorian." The sentence (or rather the sentence fragment) in question reads:

> [The] Word, that bonded itself in an entirely unique way to him, who, conceived by the Holy Spirit and born of the virgin Mary, is the second Adam. . . .[2]

The passage seems to suggest that Christ, as the human "second Adam," existed prior to the bonding to the divine Word, although his conception is said to be due to the Holy Spirit. Several years before being charged,

---

1   D.H.Th. Vollenhoven, *Schematische Kaarten*, ed. and annotated by K.A. Bril and P.J. Boonstra (Amstelveen: De Zaak Haes, 2000), 269. Nestorius (2nd half 4th century – 1st half 5th century) was condemned for emphasizing Christ's human nature to be initially disjoint from his divine nature. For a fuller description and discussion of this episode in Vollenhoven's life, see chapters 8 ["Opposing formations"] and 9 ["Vollenhoven accused"], in J. Stellingwerff, *D.H. Th. Vollenhoven (1892–1978) Reformator der Wijsbegeerte* (Baarn: Ten Have, 1992). For the relevant documents and their translations, consult the internet link of J. Glenn Friesen, www.members. shaw.ca/hermandooyeweerd/Curators.html.

2   D.H.Th. Vollenhoven, *Het Calvinisme en de Reformatie van de Wijsbegeerte* (Amsterdam: Paris, 1933), 47. The cited passage is quoted – to support the charge – in a declaration that Vollenhoven was forced to sign; see final note below.

Vollenhoven had already openly regretted his formulation and promised to revise it, should a second edition of the book appear. But to read this passage as decisive regarding the issue of a "personal" versus an "impersonal" nature of the human Christ seems entirely gratuitous. Vollenhoven in turn argued that the expression "impersonal human nature" does not occur in the main confessions of the church in connection with Christology. So to consider the denial of this to be heresy is actually out of order.

But the theological faculty, seeing the scholastic position under threat, sought to undercut Vollenhoven's popularity and growing influence and used the concern for the confessions to that end.[3] He was forced by the curators of the university to publically recant his "error" and give a full explanation in a published article.[4] To date and to its shame, the university has not exonerated (the memory of) Vollenhoven of this unjust blame and demeaning treatment.

---

3   J. Stellingwerff speaks of "jealousy" in this connection (see his *Vollenhoven*, 109). Also the initial complaint against Vollenhoven, as raised by the Theological Faculty, concerned his teaching. Vollenhoven was at that time popular as a teacher. When the theologians were asked to be more specific about the teaching objections, they came with their formal complaint as indicated.

4   The article in question is D.H.Th. Vollenhoven, "Anhypostatos," *Philosophia Reformata* 5:2 (1940): 65–79. The declaration that Vollenhoven had to sign is on page 79 of this article. See also the annotation on "anhypostatos" by K.A. Bril, in D.H.Th. Vollenhoven, *Schematische Kaarten*, 268–270.

Index

— Reformed Epistemology —

- presupposes, when speaking of "general" and "specific" in Greek thought   17, 23
- require material not content in Kant   143
- theory of, in Stoicism, signify and represent   42, 43

Concept and judgment
- and control of environment   14
- in Aristotle   35, 36
- in the Stoics   42
- judgment (truth) presupposes possession of a concept   115, 143
- sharp distinction between, in Bolzano, also in Brentano   163, 197
- Socrates began with judgment and ended with concept   15

Concept formation
- and confusion of *logos* in Augustine   60
- and method and preparatory role of intuition in inquiry   75, 204
- and speaking prophesies   158
- and supernatural domain   82
- and the directions of: complicating and simplifying   189
- as fulfilling a coherence supportive role   132, 141
- as moral in Socrates   15, 16
- as the form of lower but immanent material in Kant   143
- connecting logical schema with logical analogies in other spheres   66, 202
- in coming to know through own inquiry   75
- is system of relation-with-its-relata and a specific truth   138
- is truth(-moments) grasped in a form   15, 17, 22, 33
- moment of a thing becomes system with submoments   67, 189
- new possibility for, and more justice to, in Neoplatonism   45, 55
- new possibilities for, in modern science, also limitations   114, 115
- not characterized by individuality   17
- not preceded by judgment of intuition in Anselm   86
- not replaceable by description of spatial forms   30
- not to be modeled on approach of an object in perception   203
- relating moments of field of inquiry   114

Concrete status of both concept and truth   40, 203
Confession   87, 98
Consciousness (*see also* self-)   61, 146
Contemplation, when grasping logical schema   187
Content
- a necessary truth has "timeless" content   124
- conceiving as gasping truth-content in a truth form   33
- content of adequate concept equals truth one wishes to grasp   137
- content of concepts gained through the logical analogy   144
- Hegel adopted content of his system from Schelling   150
- in Anselm, belief of revealed content prepared by reason   86
- in Cohen contents of perception and *Ding an sich*   176
- in Cusanus, human being creates not matter but the truth of matter as content   109
- in early natural science spatial form as lacking content   112, 115
- in Franciscans, inborn content of non-logical nature   73
- in Kant, concept requires material not content   143
- in late Schelling, content called divine Father   149
- in Lotze, act and content in both representation and thought   168
- in Neoplatonism, act-content schema crossing form-material schema in human being   53
- in Plato, content of a judgment is knowledge   22
- in Rickert, content without forms are "blind"   193
- in Schelling, security of form-content schema approached from side of content   147, 148
- later content based on earlier content in order of law-spheres   66
Control   14, 17, 115, 116, 168, 209
Conversion   59
Copy, nature of representation   33
corpus christianum   95
Cosmos   94
- as willed project in Calvin   94, 212
- in Renaissance no longer divine project;

—96—

- forming content of, when not yet a
  problem 14
- in Aristotle, of subsumption; their correlation to concepts 35, 36
- its truth, in divine and human use 49
- pronouncing of (*see* Pronouncing j.)
Judgment of discerning or existence
- and pistical modality in Anselm 86
- cancelled in Socrates 16
- correlate to knowledge by intuition 20
- correlated to an intuition 16
- not identical to judgment of perception
  20, 82, 86
- not linked to a concept or to concept
  formation 15, 86
- schema of, as "A is" 36, 199
Judgment of relation
- correlate to knowledge by concepts 20,
  115
- not same as judgment of existence or
  discerning 15, 36, 82, 86
Judgment of science
- every one is synthetic but never a priori
  144
Judgment synthesis
- except in language, only in syllogism in
  Aristotle 37
- involves simple judgments 131, 199

Kant, Immanuel 130-135, 139, 141-144,
  150, 163, 171, [174], 176, 178, 193,
  203n153, 212
Katzer, E. 93n53
Kepler, Johannes 117
Knowing
- in Brentano k. and judging on a par (via
  act-content schema) 200
- in Descartes, knowing subject, again part
  of the soul 120
- is truth-possession; *systasis* not synthesis;
  condition not act 22
- when neo-idealistically understood:
  thought fashioning what intuition
  senses 194, 205
"Knowing of"
- and acts or *cogitationes* in Descartes 120
- and the "of"/"about" as prefiguring
  subject-object schema 55
- as origin of inner perception with knowledge value in Descartes 120
- starting point for Augustine 59
"Knowing that"
- and "believing that" 75

- and "knowing (of)" 22, 26, 59, 192
Knowledge
- and linguistic exchange 25
- as community of concepts, synthesized
  by thought 22
- as formed content of a judgment 14, 22
- by intuition and by concepts 20
- calls for higher standpoint 93
- conceptual/formed and non-conceptual/
  unformed 15, 19
- distinguished from truth in Bolzano
  163
- entirely immanent in Kant 143
- in Thomas, arises through abstraction
  72
- in Thomas, described as *adequatio*, not
  truth possession 72
Knowledge and perception 20, 29, 44
- never k. without p. 143
- sensorial k. in Augustine/Neoplatonism
  71
- sensorial k. not defended by Thomas 72
Knowledge of God
- in Renaissance reduced to nature as
  source 103, 104
- not equal to knowledge of relations in
  distinct regions 103
Kortmulder, Richardus Johannes 146n92
Kratylos 160
Kroner, Richard 146n91, 147n94,
  148n95, 149n95
Kuyper, Abraham 49n21, 82n48,
  100n63, 101n65, 209, 210, 211n158-
  159, 212n160

Lactantius, Lucius Caecilius Firmianus 52
Lange, Friedrich Albert 162n102-103
Language
- also supports pseudo-concept and wayward opinion 160
- l.-psychology, context of logic when
  rejecting truth-realism 68
Lasson, Adolf 162
Lasson, Georg 94n54
Law as boundary between God and cosmos 48
Law-spheres [61], 66, 120, 123
- as arranged terrains, when intuited like
  circles of consideration 61
- as well-organized book 66
- Freiburgers don't distinguish terrains of
  science 178
- law-sphere and truth identified in Lotze

- as supporting order, without being subject to law 142
- terrain high in cosmic order, capable of being investigated 142
Motion
- a basic sphere 175
- in Hegel, self-m. of truth 156
- m. of mind fashions line 111
- sensitive soul's perceptions, based in part on m. 27
- shared and not shared 117
Mysticism 107
- and regeneration 92, 93
- and *via negationis* 104
- pantheistic 12
- 7th century BC 11
Mystics, tempted by vertical higher-lower schema of Aristotle 97

Name and concept 42, 43
Napoleon Bonaparte 76
Natorp, Paul 175n124, 177
Natural science
- becomes mathematical when numbers are intra-mental 112
Negation, the uncompleted combination of form and content 35, 160, 166
Neo-Kantianism 123, 191
Neoplatonic influences in Augustine 59
Neoplatonists/-ism 53, 55, 56, [57], 60, 71, 80, 102, 110, 141
Newton, Isaac 174
Nietzsche, Friedrich Wilhelm 13
Nominalism
- and language 68
- in Stoicism focuses on denial of substantiality of general concepts 43
- in Thomas, struggle between realism and n. 69
Norm is a measure; not suited to secure value 182
Norm and pronouncing of judgment 187 (*see also* pronouncing judgment)
Norm, command and law, confusion between 179
Norms secure values according to Rickert 181, 192
Non-being [*me on*] 109, 146
Non-logical, not same as truth about it, or same as a-cosmic 115
Nous
- passive and active in Aristotle 27, 71
- passive and active in Thomas 72

Number
- and mind 24
- and modality 201
- world of, first law-sphere following upon the logos 112
Nuzubidse, Schalwa 35n14, 207

Object as felt resistance of active subject 14
Object of perception 16, 17, 18, 20, 33, 67, 115, 120, 121, 125, 200
Objects immanent to mind confuse judgment with concept 115
Oesterreich, Traugott Konstantin 156n98, 162n105, 165n110, 168n114
Offices of religion and election 97, 98
- o. and capacities of willing and cognition in Calvin 98
- prophetic o. 98
Oken, Lorenz 168
One in Neoplatonism 53, 54
Order, cosmic 23, 24, 111, 112, 142, 153, 203
Order, mechanical 123
Order of God 137, 211, 222
Order of the mind 109, 141
Ordinances or laws as chief partition 9
Organon of thought 49
- intuited schema of logical law-sphere 49
Origen 49, 51, 56

Pan-teleological system 34, 81
Particular 17, 18, 23, 40, 123, 203
Pascal, Blaise 122, 224
Paul (the Apostle) 122
Perceive(r)
- as soul in free relation to model 33
- characterized by individuality 17
- creates free reproductions of the perceived 17
- in Descartes method of physics linked to what is perceptible 120
- Malebranche's seeing all things in God 121
- perceived thing is only correlate of p. 117
- to p. is not the same as to know 20
- whole personality active in both knowing and perceiving 115
Perception
- as check in science 115

198
Psychical
- "believing that" as the ps. correlate of
  communication 87
- distinction of the ps. and the *logos* is
  vital 207
- distinction perception and representation
  in Husserl by way of the ps. 203
- "knowledge of" is ps. 22
- no interest in ps. connections between
  representations in Kant 142
- organon of concept formation does not
  belong to matters ps. 198
- psychical activity and logical factor together 173
- psychical coherence in Husserl's triadic
  schema 202
- psychical moment wrongfully called
  true 60
- understanding and ps. activity 155, 173
Psychological/-gy
- Bolzano psychologically transcends Descartes 165
- Brentano: everything psychological intends 197
- difference between dialectics and rhetoric
  is
- psychological 42
- in Brentano form is psychically active
  200
- in Franciscan school more inborn than
  just psychologized logical form 73
- independence of psychology threatened
  by mechanics 126
- logic, when lacking the character of
  truth, regressed to language psychology 68
- Natorp: Reflecting on primary experience is to do psychology 177
- psychological dominance of physics
  120
- psychological meaning of a priori 134,
  135
- psychology and phenomenology in Husserl 202
- psychology, basis for novel connection
  of subject-object schema and form-
  matter 53
- psychology in Descartes 120
- psychology in Hegel banal 153
Psychologism
- in Augustine, "knowing" more than
  naïve ps. 61

- *reductio ad absurdum* argument against
  individualistic psychologism 202
Pure Ego 192
Pyramid of form-matter metaphysics 26,
  53
- and divinity in Augustine 80
- in pyramid structure humanity equated
  with general church 81, 95
- pyramid structure falls through in Calvin 95
- pyramid structure, no place for church in
  Kuyper's view 209
- pyramid structure occasioning pantheistic blurring of boundary 73
- useless figure in connection with truth
  66

Ranke, Leopold 181
Ratio, not synonymous with concept 155
Ratio: requires subject connected to the
  logical schema 154
Rationalism vs. empiricism: failure to separate knowledge and perception 118
- its combined cognitively purified knowledge and overrating of subject 119
Real
- r. and unreal in Brentano 198
- r. concept possessed by mind when pronouncing judgment 115
- r. content and logical form replace contingent and necessary in Kant 131
Realism
- in extreme r., universals still not seen as
  things 67
- in Thomas half-hearted 69
Realist
- from r. standpoint, thought is never
  spontaneous, though it is active 173
- r. adage "*universale ante rem*" 66
- r.-Aristotelian classification of living-dead
  as higher-lower 126
- Rickert does violence to every realist
  division 185
Reality
- Calvinist and the ideal and r. 211
- degrees of, in Neoplatonism 53, 59
- Husserl excludes questions of factual
  r. 203
- in biotic sense, not essence, in physical
  not appearance 32
- in Rickert r. is idealistically transformed
  facts of the positivists 186
- of truth, depends only on its own char-

- in Husserl evidenced by biologistic phenotype epistemology 205
- in Husserl, in his equating order-
theoretical apriority and generality of
concepts 203
- in late s. status of theology as science
disputable 89
- influence on s. of Augustine and Thomas
differs greatly 79
- its wrongly posed problem of relation of
religion and theology 77-78
- often not appreciated, yet here too revelation of God 62, 63
- views essence and object of perception as
(hidden) inner psyche and outer body
67, 68
Schouten, W.J.A. 117n74
Schwann, Theodore 168
Science
- a task high but limited 210
- new aim of special science: determining
relations between moments 114, 128
- new concept of, contra to teleology and
Platonic dualism 117
- task of humankind 77, 128, 183
Sciences, free grouping of, no more possible than for law-spheres 188
Scientific method, correlated to a circle of
consideration 126
Scotus, Duns 89
Scripture, anthropomorphic about God,
non-anthropomorphic about cosmos
51
- S's threefold sense in Origen 51
Scripture revelation 92, 209
- S. revelation: what prophets communicate to the church 92
Security connection for circles of consideration 126, 132, 141, 142
- s.c. and humanistic standpoint 142
Sein und Sollen
- in Kant and Kantianism 142
Self
- as ultimate foundation in supporting
arrangement 144, 145
- in absolute idealism creates knowledge,
but itself thereby s. unknowable 146
Self-consciousness
- as hypostatized, the immaterial form of
Aristotle's pyramid 26
- nous matter to divine form of s. in Aristotle 27, 38
- the One of Neoplatonisms more elevated

than s. 53
- in Neoplatonism denied deification 54
Semi-idealism 162, 166
- of Thomas Aquinas in Husserl 206
Sense-perception
- and functioning organs 46
- broader than knowledge 115
Sensibility 143, 162, 166, 193
- forms of 132, 143, 166, 176
Sensualism, in Bolzano 167
Sermo-theory 68
Significance 42, 164
Sigwart, Christoph 170
Simplifying method 189
Sin, as transgression of law 48
Skepticism, in consequence of self-divination 47
- s. and faith in Tertullian and Lactantius
52
- s. and scholasticism 90
- unavoidable when perception affords
knowledge 120
Socrates 14, 15, 16, 18
Sophists 14, 15
Soul
- as center of individual substance
(monad) in Leibniz 123
- as dreaming, a phase of the subjective
spirit in Hegel 152
- as undergoing the world process of the
logos in Heraclitus 13
- as whole personality present in perception (aimed as a body) and knowing
(aimed at truth) 33, 115
- in Calvin, church as s. of the Christian
body 95
- in concept formation, grasping a truth-
content in a truth-form 33, 55
- in Descartes includes knowing subject
120
- in mysticism s. only half divine 107
- in perception and work of representation, focused on matter 33, 115
- in Renaissance humans s. reveals itself as
designer and is idealized 101, 110
- in work of reproduction, follows model
33
- kinds of, in Aristotle 27
- means by which truth is intuited, the
organ of divine experience 60
- tarrying impressions raise general representations on the s. 28
- when used by s. logical form still has a

www.ingramcontent.com/pod-product-compliance
Lightning Source LLC
LaVergne TN
LVHW091258080426
835510LV00007B/306